P9-EDJ-690

DATE DUE

JUN 1 1981			
OCT 2 1989			
GAYLORD 234			PRINTED IN U. S. A.

L.I.F.E. College Library
1100 Glendale Blvd.
Los Angeles, Calif. 90026

SECOND THOUGHTS ON THE DEAD SEA SCROLLS

Other works by F. F. Bruce

THE DAWN OF CHRISTIANITY

THE GROWING DAY

LIGHT IN THE WEST

THE ACTS OF THE APOSTLES: GREEK TEXT WITH INTRODUCTION AND COMMENTARY

THE BOOK OF THE ACTS: ENGLISH TEXT WITH EXPOSITION AND NOTES

THE BOOKS AND THE PARCHMENTS

ARE THE NEW TESTAMENT DOCUMENTS RELIABLE?

THE HITTITES AND THE OLD TESTAMENT

WADI QUMRAN, LOOKING TOWARDS THE DEAD SEA

The commencement of the hills containing the caves can be seen at the top right-hand of the picture.

AT KHIRBET QUMRAN

Cave 1 appears at the top left-hand of the picture. In the foreground are the remains of a kiln, used apparently for baking bread.

SECOND THOUGHTS ON THE DEAD SEA SCROLLS

by

F. F. BRUCE, M.A.

Professor of Biblical History and Literature in the University of Sheffield

5673

LONDON:
THE PATERNOSTER PRESS
1956

L.I.F.E. College Library
1100 Glendale Blvd.
Los Angeles 26, Calif.

ALL RIGHTS RESERVED

First Published . . . 1956

Copyright U.S.A., 1956, by
The Paternoster Press

Made and Printed in Great Britain
for The Paternoster Press 11 Great
James Street Bedford Row London
W.C.1 by Wyman & Sons Limited
London Fakenham and Reading

221.4
B83s

LIFE Pacific College
Alumni Library
1100 West Covina Blvd.
San Dimas, CA 91773

TO MY STUDENTS
IN THE UNIVERSITY OF SHEFFIELD
WHO TEACH ME
NEARLY AS MUCH
AS I TEACH THEM

CONTENTS

		PAGE
	Preface	9
	Prologue	11
CHAPTER		
I.	The First Discoveries	15
II.	Later Discoveries	26
III.	Dating the Finds	34
IV.	Khirbet Qumran	45
V.	Wadi Murabba'at and Khirbet Mird	53
VI.	The Scrolls and the Old Testament	58
VII.	Biblical Interpretation and the Messianic Hope	70
VIII.	The Teacher of Righteousness and His Enemies	85
IX.	The Qumran Community	99
X.	Qumran and the Essenes	112
XI.	Qumran and Christianity	123
	Epilogue	138
	Index	141

PREFACE

SOME years ago I wrote a little book entitled *The Dawn of Christianity*—published in Great Britain as a volume in "The Second Thoughts Library" and in the United States as Part I of *The Spreading Flame*. I cannot find in it any reference to the Dead Sea Scrolls. News of the Scrolls was slowly being released at the time when that book was being written, but at that time it did not seem likely that the new knowledge would make much of a contribution to the study of Christian origins. Today the situation is quite different. In the eyes of many, the new discoveries have brought about a revolution in our understanding of Christian origins. Those who have appeared slow to admit this revolution have been reproved for their unseemly conservatism, which has been put down to religious inhibition. "It is difficult," says one writer, "for the clergyman scholar to face certain implications of the contents of the Dead Sea manuscripts." He himself, we are to assume, is eager only to follow truth wherever it may lead. But so, we may be sure, is the "clergyman scholar" whom he criticizes.

Whether the following pages are the work of a scholar is for others to judge. But it cannot be urged against them that they are the work of a clergyman. A lay teacher in a secular university will perhaps be allowed some freedom from those inhibitions which are alleged to beset his ordained colleagues—but one never knows. Yet this may be said at the outset. If *The Dawn of Christianity* were being written now, instead of seven years ago, it would no doubt be a much better book (for it would benefit by the added experience and, we hope, wisdom of these seven years), and it would certainly contain copious references to the Dead Sea Scrolls. But the second thoughts induced by the Scrolls would affect only incidental features of the story. The main point of view would be defended all the more confidently and vigorously because of these new discoveries.

The title of this book, then, is not *Second Thoughts on the Dawn of Christianity* but *Second Thoughts on the Dead Sea Scrolls.* For as more and more information comes to hand about these documents, earlier estimates of their significance have to be revised. Indeed, the word "second" in the title must be interpreted in a liberal sense. Some of the thoughts which find expression here are probably third, fourth or even fifth thoughts. But they are certainly not last thoughts.

Yet the outlines of the situation out of which these documents emerged are becoming increasingly clear; and unless some quite incalculable factor is suddenly introduced into the picture, it seems likely that further information, as it continues to be published, will modify a number of points here and there but in general will help to fill the outlines in and make them clearer rather than necessitate a radical reinterpretation.

I have tried to maintain a clear distinction between the new evidence itself and the inferences which I think should be drawn from it. I hope I have succeeded in this.

My grateful acknowledgments are due to Mr. David J. Ellis, of King's College, London, who has provided the frontispiece and illustration for dust wrapper, to Mr. David F. Payne, of the Hebrew University, Jerusalem, for the description of Masada quoted on pp. 50 f., and to my wife, for her help at every stage of the work.

September, 1956 F. F. Bruce

PROLOGUE

WHEN the Persian king Cyrus brought the Babylonian Empire to an end in 539 B.C., he authorized a body of Jewish displaced persons to return to their home in Judæa, from which they had been deported by Nebuchadrezzar two generations previously, and to rebuild their national shrine in Jerusalem. After some years the temple was rebuilt, and its services were carried out anew by the members of the old priestly families, at whose head stood Jeshua, a scion of the house of Zadok, which had occupied the chief priesthood in the former temple since its dedication by King Solomon about 960 B.C. down to its destruction by the Babylonians in 587. But, while the ancient chief-priestly family was restored to its sacred office, the royal house of David, which also returned from exile, was not restored to the kingship.

The new Jewish community was organized as a temple-state, consisting of Jerusalem and a few miles around. At the head of the state was the high priest, who controlled internal Jewish affairs; the wider interests of the Persian Empire were the responsibility of the civil governor of Judæa, who was appointed by the crown. When, after two hundred years, the Persian Empire was in its turn brought to an end by Alexander the Great, no material change took place in the Jewish constitution. They had a Macedonian governor over them instead of one appointed by the Persian king; they had to pay taxes to a Macedonian court instead of to the Persian court; they were exposed to the powerful influence of Hellenistic culture. But the high priests of the house of Zadok remained as before at the head of the Jewish temple-state. So matters continued under the domination of the Ptolemies, who inherited Alexander's empire in Egypt, and retained Palestine under their control until 198 B.C. When in that year they lost Palestine to the rival dynasty of the Seleucids, who had succeeded to Alexander's heritage in the greater part of Asia, the transition was smooth so far as Judæa was concerned. To be sure, the increasing tendency to follow western ways caused grave concern to the more conservatively-minded Jews, but they had no complaint against the Gentile government, which guaranteed the temple constitution and granted the utmost liberty in the practice of the Jewish religion.

For a variety of reasons a change came about with the accession of Antiochus IV (Epiphanes) to the Seleucid throne in 175 B.C. Early in his reign he interfered with the Zadokite succession to the high priesthood; later he tried to prohibit the Jewish religion altogether. This led to a national and religious rising, as a result of which Judæa ultimately secured complete political independence. The leaders of this rising, the priestly family of the Hasmoneans, became the ruling dynasty in the independent state, and assumed the high priesthood in addition to the chief civil and military power. From 142 to 63 B.C. the Jews preserved their hardly won independence under the Hasmoneans, but in the latter year they lost it to the Romans, who reorganized all the territory west of the Euphrates as part of their empire. But the Romans left a Hasmonean high priest in charge of the internal affairs of Judæa for over twenty years. In 40 B.C., however, the political situation in western Asia caused them to nominate one Herod as king of the Jews, and Herod ruled Palestine from 37 to 4 B.C. in the interests of Rome. His son Archelaus, who succeeded him in Judæa, was deposed by the Roman Emperor in A.D. 6, and for the next sixty years Judæa was governed by procurators appointed by the Emperor, except for three years (A.D. 41–44) when a grandson of Herod, Agrippa I, reigned over Judæa as king. From the beginning of Herod's reign the high priests, who were henceforth appointed by Herod and his descendants, or else by Roman governors, counted for less and less, although by virtue of their office they continued to preside over the Sanhedrin, the supreme court of the Jewish nation.

Misrule by Roman procurators, combined with an increasing intolerance of Gentile control on the part of Jewish nationalists, led to the Jewish revolt of A.D. 66 and the destruction of the city and temple of Jerusalem by the Roman forces in A.D. 70. With the fall of the temple, the last vestiges of the temple constitution, together with the high-priestly office, came to an end. Judæa was placed under firmer military control than before. But in A.D. 132 a new revolt broke out, and the independence of Judæa was proclaimed under a messianic claimant who is commonly known as Bar-Kokhba. After three years of guerrilla fighting this rising was crushed. Jerusalem was rebuilt by the Romans as a completely Gentile city, and a new chapter opened in the history of the Holy Land.

This sketch of Israel's political fortunes under the Persians, Greeks and Romans may provide a framework within which we may get our bearings more easily when we consider the situation which produced the Dead Sea Scrolls.

CHAPTER I

THE FIRST DISCOVERIES

What are the Dead Sea Scrolls?

THEY are manuscripts which have come to light from time to time since the spring of 1947 in a number of areas lying north-west of the Dead Sea. But while we concentrate our attention on these recent discoveries—exciting and important as they are—it is worth remembering that other finds of a similar nature have been made in the same region at much earlier times. We shall have occasion to say something about these earlier discoveries later on,[1] but the discoveries of our own day began by accident when a goatherd of the Bedouin tribe of Ta'amireh, Muhammad adh-Dhib ("Muhammad the Wolf") by name, was grazing a herd of goats in the neighbourhood of the Dead Sea, and in a cave near the Wadi Qumran came upon a long-forgotten storehouse of Hebrew and Aramaic documents. Accounts of his adventure differ in detail, but this is how it was described in *The Times* of August 9, 1949, by Mr. G. Lankester Harding, Director of Antiquities in the Hashemite Kingdom of Jordan:

> One of the goats strayed in search for better pastures, and the goatherd, looking for it up the steep rock hillside, chanced upon a small circular opening in a rock face. With pardonable curiosity he looked in cautiously, but could make out only a large dark cavern; so he picked up a stone and threw it in—and heard something crack and break. Nervously apprehensive at the unexpected result of his effort he withdrew, and returned later with a friend. Each made brave by the presence of the other, they wriggled through the small aperture into the cavern, and in the dim light could distinguish some large jars standing on the floor, one of them broken by the recently thrown stone. Fragments of others were lying all around, but they quickly proceeded to examine the contents of the intact jars.
>
> Instead, however, of the expected golden treasure they drew forth a number of leather rolls covered in, to them, an unknown writing—had they but known it, a treasure far greater than any gold.

[1] See pp. 109 ff.

Muhammad and one or two of his friends took the rolls to Bethlehem and attempted to sell them there. After a few months, some of the rolls were acquired by the Syrian Orthodox Monastery of St. Mark, in the Old City of Jerusalem; others were secured for the Hebrew University. It is said that the manuscripts were first brought to the Syrians because a Muslim sheikh in Bethlehem, to whom they were shown, saw at a glance that the writing was not Arabic and thought that it was a form of Syriac script. The Syrian Archbishop of Jerusalem, Athanasius Yeshue Samuel, recognized that the writing was Hebrew, but neither he nor his colleagues were able to determine the nature and significance of the documents. The Archbishop therefore consulted several scholars in Jerusalem who might be expected to advise him. Late in July, 1947, a few weeks after his monastery had bought the manuscripts, he consulted a member of the *École Biblique*, a splendid institution for Biblical and archaeological study in Jerusalem manned by French Dominicans. At this time an eminent Dutch scholar, Professor J. van der Ploeg, of Nijmegen University, was giving a course of lectures in the *École Biblique*, and he was taken to see the manuscripts at the Syrian monastery. He identified one of them as a copy of the Book of Isaiah in Hebrew, apparently of astonishingly early date, but when he reported what he had seen to his friends at the *École Biblique*, one scholar of outstanding authority in this field of study told him that it was preposterous to suppose that Hebrew manuscripts of such antiquity could exist, and that the scrolls he had seen must be fakes. Accordingly Professor van der Ploeg thought no more of the matter for the time being. (Before long, the scholars of the *École Biblique* found reason to change their minds, and no institution has exerted itself more nobly in the acquisition and study of the Dead Sea manuscripts. But at the time their scepticism was both natural and wise.)

The Syrians then approached members of the Jewish community in Jerusalem; after all, Jews might be expected to have a special interest in ancient Hebrew documents. Two librarians from the Hebrew University visited the monastery, but did not feel themselves capable of passing an opinion on what they saw, and suggested that an expert in palaeography from the University should be given an opportunity of examining the scrolls.

Towards the end of November, Professor Eleazar L. Sukenik,

of the Chair of Palestinian Archaeology in the Hebrew University, who had recently returned from America, bought for the University most of the remainder of the manuscripts which had originally been taken from the cave, together with two jars in which some of the manuscripts were said to have been found. At this time he did not know of the companion manuscripts which the Syrian monastery had acquired, and when at last he heard of them, it was almost impossible for him to see them. These were the closing months of the British mandatory régime in Palestine, when tension between the Jews and Arabs was mounting rapidly, and there could be no coming and going between the Jewish and Arab areas of Jerusalem and its neighbourhood. Meanwhile Sukenik was examining the documents which he had acquired. He thought they must have come from some ancient *genizah*—a storeplace in which Jews deposited sacred writings which had become too dilapidated for ordinary use, until they could be reverently disposed of. And the more he examined them, the more his excitement increased. Two days after he made his first purchase, he wrote in his diary: "I read a little more in the 'parchments.' I'm afraid of going too far in thinking about them. It may be that this is one of the greatest finds ever made in Palestine, a find we never so much as hoped for." Shortly before Christmas he was able to buy another piece of manuscript, in very poor condition. The President of the Hebrew University, Dr. Judah L. Magnes, readily saw to it that funds were made available for the purchase of the scrolls, and another colleague, Professor J. Biberkraut, undertook the delicate task of unfolding them, all crumpled, decomposing and brittle as they were.

At last, about the end of January, 1948, a meeting was arranged between Sukenik and a member of the Syrian community in the Y.M.C.A. building of Jerusalem, which was situated in one of the security zones established by the mandatory government. Sukenik was shown some of the scrolls from the monastery and allowed to borrow them for a few days. From one of them, a manuscript of the Book of Isaiah, he copied several chapters for his own interest. On February 6 he returned the scrolls, and arrangements were made for another meeting at which it was hoped the Syrian Archbishop and the President of the University would both be present, to arrange for the purchase of the scrolls by the University. But this meeting never took place.

The British mandatory government in Palestine came to an end on May 15, 1948, and in the trouble that ensued Jerusalem was divided between the two sides—the Jews and the Arabs. The Syrian monastery was in the Arab zone, and when once the fighting broke out there could be no easy communication between that zone and the Jewish zone. When, some months later, the Constituent Assembly of the State of Israel met, each member found on his desk a copy of Isa. 40 as transcribed by Sukenik from the Syrian scroll, together with an account of the scroll and notes on the text, comparing it with the traditional text. Certainly no more propitious words could have been found for the occasion than the prophet's message of consolation: "Comfort ye, comfort ye my people, saith your God."

But we are going ahead too quickly. On Wednesday afternoon, February 18, 1948, Mr. John C. Trever, Acting Director of the American School of Oriental Research in Jerusalem, was called to the telephone to hear something about ancient Hebrew manuscripts. Somewhat sceptically, he went to find that the speaker at the other end was a priest of the Syrian monastery, Father Butros Sowmy. Father Sowmy told him that "while working in the library of the Convent, cataloguing the books, he had come upon five scrolls in ancient Hebrew about which their catalogue contained no information." Remembering an earlier pleasant contact with members of the American School, he thought that they might be able to give some help in this matter.

Accordingly next day Father Sowmy and his brother, a civil servant, called at the American School with a suitcase containing five scrolls (or parts of scrolls) wrapped in newspaper, and a smaller fragment of manuscript. As cameras were not available at the moment, Mr. Trever copied some lines of the largest scroll by hand. While he was doing so, his visitors told him that the documents had really come, not from the monastery library, but from a cave near the north end of the Dead Sea, where they had been found by Bedouin.

Mr. Trever soon came to the conclusion that the Hebrew script of the scrolls was more archaic than anything of the kind he had ever seen. When his visitors left, he examined the words which he had transcribed, and was not long in recognizing part of the Hebrew text of the Book of Isaiah. Next day he visited the monastery (obtaining access to the Old City of Jerusalem through the Jaffa Gate with some difficulty), and persuaded Archbishop Samuel to allow the scrolls to be photographed at the American School. They were brought to the school for this purpose on February 21, and a beginning was made with the work of photographing them. One of the scrolls, however, was badly damaged and proved so difficult to unroll that it was decided to wait until it could be taken to some place where it could be unrolled without causing further damage. From some of the writing that was visible, it appeared that this scroll was written, not in Hebrew, but in a sister-language, Aramaic.

As soon as possible, the plates were developed and a few prints from the Isaiah scroll were sent by air-mail to Professor W. F. Albright, of Johns Hopkins University, Baltimore—perhaps the most eminent figure among living Biblical archaeologists. Professor Albright sent an air-letter by return post, in which he said:

> My heartiest congratulations on the greatest manuscript discovery of modern times! There is no doubt in my mind that the script is more archaic than that of the Nash Papyrus. . . . I should prefer a date around 100 B.C. . . . What an absolutely incredible find! And there can happily not be the slightest doubt in the world about the genuineness of the manuscript.

Professor Albright's excitement may be readily understood when we remember that at that time no Biblical manuscripts in Hebrew were known to survive much, if at all, earlier in date than the ninth century A.D. Therefore, if he was right in dating this manuscript of Isaiah around 100 B.C., it meant that the interval separating the time at which the books of the Old Testament were originally written from the time at which the oldest extant Hebrew copies were made was suddenly reduced by about a thousand years. The Nash Papyrus, which he mentioned in his letter, is a Hebrew fragment in Cambridge University Library containing the Ten Commandments, followed by the words: "The statutes and the judgments which Moses commanded the [children of Israel] in the wilderness when they came out of the land of Egypt: 'Hear, O Israel, the LORD our God is one LORD, and thou shalt love [the LORD] thy God with all thy heart . . .'" This papyrus had been variously dated from the second century A.D. back to the first century B.C. (Professor Albright himself preferring the earlier dating); but in any case, if the newly discovered manuscript was older than the Nash Papyrus, the implications of the find were revolutionary. Professor Albright's confidence that the genuineness of the manuscript was beyond doubt was to be fully confirmed, but we may wonder how he could be so sure at that early stage in events, when he had only photographs to go by.

On the last day of February the Director of the American School, Dr. Millar Burrows, returned from Iraq, where he had been for two weeks. His interest was immediately captivated by the new discoveries, and he used one of the documents as the subject-matter for the remaining part of a course in epigraphy which he was conducting at the school. He told Archbishop Samuel what his judgment was on the antiquity of the scrolls, saying that the Isaiah scroll was, in his belief, the oldest known manuscript of any book of the Bible. The Archbishop was deeply impressed by this information—how deeply may be judged by the fact that within a week he had sent the scrolls to a place of safety outside Palestine. To export antiquities from Palestine without a permit from the Department of Antiquities was illegal, although the imminent break-down of an effective central authority in the land might be pleaded in extenuation.

Early in 1949 Archbishop Samuel arrived in the United States with his precious documents. He handed them over for a period of three years to the American Schools of Oriental Research, who undertook to publish their contents. It should be explained here that the American Schools of Oriental Research are two in number —one in Jerusalem and one at Baghdad—and that the American headquarters of the Schools are at New Haven, Connecticut. Dr. Burrows' period of office as Director of the Jerusalem School came to an end in the spring of 1948, and he was now back in Yale University, where he holds the Winkley Chair of Biblical Theology. He and his colleagues, Dr. Trever and Dr. W. H. Brownlee, now gave themselves to the task of preparing the scrolls for publication. As originally acquired by the Syrian monastery, the scrolls were five in number, but it soon appeared that there were in reality only four, as what had seemed to be two turned out to be severed halves of one original scroll (the scroll commonly referred to as the *Manual of Discipline*, but more accurately called the *Rule of the Community*).

Three of the scrolls were published in facsimile and transcription with admirable promptitude.[1] The fourth, however, which could not be unrolled for photographing in Jerusalem, continued to resist attempts to unroll it. Preparations were well advanced, however, for treating the material in a manner that would enable it to be unrolled without irreparable damage, when the agreed period for which the Archbishop had granted the American Schools custody of the scrolls expired. Despite pleas to let them retain the fourth scroll a little longer, he insisted on taking all four of them back.

Now that the world of learning had sufficient information about the nature of the scrolls, it was hoped that some institution would be prepared to buy them. But—partly, no doubt, because of uncertainty about their legal ownership—universities and libraries were reluctant to make an offer for them. They were actually advertised for sale in the "Miscellaneous" columns of the *Wall Street Journal* in June, 1954. At length, on February 13, 1955, it was announced that they had been bought for the State of Israel, the price paid being two hundred and fifty thousand dollars. The money is to be used for religious and educational work in connexion with the Syrian Orthodox Church.

Thus, nearly eight years after the discovery, the two lots of scrolls were reunited under the same owners. The Premier of Israel announced that a special museum would be built to house the newly acquired manuscripts, together with those purchased previously for the Hebrew University, and that it would be known as the Shrine of the Book.

What were these Documents?

Let us take the four acquired by the Syrian Monastery first. One of them, as has already been said, was a copy of the Book of Isaiah in Hebrew. Another was a copy of the first two chapters of the Book of Habakkuk in Hebrew, accompanied by something like a verse-by-verse commentary, also in Hebrew. The third—the one which had been torn in two—proved to be the text of a code of rules or "manual of discipline" of some Jewish religious

[1] *The Dead Sea Scrolls of St. Mark's Monastery*, edited by Millar Burrows. Volume I: *The Isaiah Manuscript and the Habakkuk Commentary* (1950). Volume II, Fascicle 2: *Plates and Transcription of the Manual of Discipline* (1951).

community. We shall call it the *Rule of the Community*. The fourth was early seen to be written in Aramaic, and not in Hebrew like the other three. It was not unrolled until after its purchase by the State of Israel. Quite soon after the scrolls were brought to America by Archbishop Samuel, Dr. John Trever suggested that it was probably a copy of the Book of Lamech, an apocryphal work mentioned in one or two ancient lists. His reason for thinking this was that a detached fragment of the scroll contained a sentence in which Lamech, the father of Noah, speaks in the first person and mentions his wife Bit'enosh.[1] But when news was released of the unrolling and deciphering of this fourth scroll in February, 1956, it was announced that it was not the Book of Lamech, but an expanded Aramaic paraphrase of Chapters 5 to 15 of the Book of Genesis, in which not only Lamech, but other leading figures in the narrative of Genesis (*e.g.* Abraham), tell their part of the story in the first person.

The scrolls bought by Professor Sukenik in November and December, 1947, turned out to be three in number,[2] although one of them was in four pieces. This was a collection of hymns of thanksgiving, most of which open with the words: "I give thee thanks, O Lord, because . . ." Another was a most interesting work which Sukenik named *The War of the Children of Light with the Children of Darkness*. (We shall refer to it by its own shorter title, the *Rule of War*.) He loved to tell how, as he pored over this description of ancient warfare in the dark days of 1948, when shells were flying over Jerusalem, he had difficulty at times in distinguishing between the contemporary reality and the remote situation pictured in the scroll he was studying. The third scroll which he acquired was another copy of Isaiah, of which the text from Chapter 41 onwards was reasonably complete, while that of the earlier chapters had survived only in about a dozen fragments. All three of these documents were in Hebrew.

More will be said about each of them later on. But we have already seen why such importance was attached to them right from the time when their discovery was announced. If the date

[1] Bit'enosh is also given as the name of Lamech's wife in *The Book of Jubilees*, another expanded paraphrase of Genesis, composed in the second century B.C. See p. 89.

[2] His edition of them was published posthumously in Jerusalem: *The Dead Sea Scrolls of the Hebrew University* (1955).

first assigned to them by men like Professors Albright, Burrows, and Sukenik could be established as correct, it meant that manuscripts of the Hebrew Scriptures had come to light which were older by at least a thousand years than any hitherto known. Such a claim of antiquity was naturally received with considerable scepticism. The possibility of any such discovery had been generally discounted. Old Testament textual scholars had, for the most part, resigned themselves to the indefinite acceptance of the millennial gap dividing the date of the oldest surviving copies of Hebrew Scripture from the date at which the latest parts of Hebrew Scripture were originally composed. (And the oldest parts of Hebrew Scripture were originally composed another millennium earlier still.) No less an authority than Sir Frederic Kenyon had written in *Our Bible and the Ancient Manuscripts*: "There is, indeed, no probability that we shall ever find manuscripts of the Hebrew text going back to a period before the formation of the text which we know as Massoretic"[1]—and in the last edition of the book, published in 1939, that statement was allowed to remain (p. 48), for it represented the consensus of informed opinion then as much as it had done when the first edition appeared in 1895. Yet, less than ten years after the publication of the last edition, the situation was completely changed; and Kenyon himself, before his death on August 23, 1952, accepted and welcomed the reading of the new discoveries which carried the textual evidence for Hebrew Scripture a thousand years further back. Even before the new evidence came to light, Kenyon believed the Massoretic text of the Old Testament to be a trustworthy representation of what the authors had written; he lived long enough to see his belief confirmed by testimony of a kind which had hardly been thought possible.

But it was thought by several scholars that those who had so promptly assigned this early dating to the manuscripts were too hasty. Sceptical voices were raised, and it was right and proper

[1] This is the text produced by the Massoretes, editors of the Hebrew text in the schools of Palestine and Babylonia in the eighth and ninth centuries A.D., who recorded the traditional pronunciation, punctuation and interpretation of the Old Testament writings. We do, however, have evidence of another kind for the text of the Old Testament in the pre-Massoretic period; for example, manuscripts of the Septuagint (the pre-Christian Greek translation of the Old Testament) have survived which antedate the earliest extant copies of the Massoretic text by six centuries and more. I have given some account of this subject in *The Books and the Parchments*, pp. 112 ff.

that scepticism should be expressed. Memories were revived of famous hoaxes; some recalled, for example, the case of a Jerusalem antiquarian named Shapira, who in the eighteen-eighties had professed to discover an ancient copy of the Book of Deuteronomy, dated about 900 B.C., which he tried to sell to the British Museum for a million pounds! Shapira's claim impressed a number of people, until it was subjected to remorseless scrutiny by a distinguished French archaeologist, Charles Simon Clermont-Ganneau, who proved that Shapira had written the copy himself on wide margins cut from synagogue scrolls, imitating the script of the then recently discovered Moabite Stone! In another field of study it was remembered how in the nineteen-twenties an Italian's claim to have discovered the lost writings of the Roman historian Livy succeeded for a time in deceiving an eminent English Latinist.

Such claims demand the most sceptical examination. If they are false, the sooner they are exposed the better. If they are valid, their validity will be all the more securely established if they have stood the severest tests. There is a genuine scepticism which St. Paul has recommended to us in the words: "Test everything; hold fast what is good" (I Thess. 5: 21). And this genuine scepticism which tests everything is an ally to true faith, not an enemy.

In America a distinguished Jewish scholar, Dr. Solomon Zeitlin of Philadelphia, has over the years ventilated almost every argument that could conceivably be urged against the antiquity of the scrolls in the *Jewish Quarterly Review*, of which he is editor.[1] (It must be immediately added that he has, with admirable impartiality, extended the hospitality of its pages to defenders of the scrolls' antiquity.) No English scholar has gone to such lengths as Dr. Zeitlin. But when the first announcements of the discovery were made, Professor Godfrey R. Driver of Oxford played a salutary part in exposing the weaknesses of some arguments adduced in support of the antiquity of the scrolls, and in demanding the most incontrovertible evidence for claims which he thought were being too lightly advanced.[2] Questions like the character of the ruling and the composition of the ink should be investigated,

[1] He has now summed up his criticisms in a monograph, *The Dead Sea Scrolls and Modern Scholarship* (1956).

[2] See, *e.g.*, his lecture to the Friends of Dr. Williams's Library, *The Hebrew Scrolls* (1950).

he urged, to test the conclusions which the palaeographers had announced. He did not *deny* the earlier dating, but he thought that those who adhered to it should bear other possibilities in mind. More recently he has acknowledged that the scrolls bear witness to a text of the Old Testament "which (whatever date is assigned to them) is older by many centuries than our Massoretic text."[1]

[1] *Hibbert Journal*, October, 1955, p. 105.

CHAPTER II

LATER DISCOVERIES

The First Cave

It was plainly of great importance that the cave where the manuscripts were said to have been found should be visited as soon as possible by an impartial commission of investigators, competent to assess the various lines of evidence. Dr. Burrows tells[1] how he and his colleagues at the American School tried to arrange a visit in March, 1948, but the arrangements fell through. Soon after that, fighting broke out between the Arab states and Israel, and a visit was out of the question so long as hostilities lasted. When at last a truce was called to the fighting, and the frontier between the opposing sides was patrolled by United Nations observers, the northern half of the western shore of the Dead Sea lay within the territory of the newly extended Hashemite Kingdom of Jordan. Thanks to the help of a Belgian officer among the United Nations observers, Captain Philippe Lippens, who was personally interested in the discovery of the scrolls, it was possible for a party to visit and inspect the cave in February, 1949. Mr. G. Lankester Harding, the Director of Antiquities for Jordan, took charge of the excavation of the cave, with the co-operation of Father Roland de Vaux, of the Dominican *École Biblique*.

It was immediately evident that they had been forestalled by other investigators, who found their way to the cave in November or December, 1948, cut a more convenient opening into it, lower than that through which the Bedouin goatherd had first entered, dug up the floor of the cave and threw some of the débris out through the new entrance. This inexpert excavation destroyed much of the evidence which the official party might otherwise have found and interpreted. One of the unofficial investigators left a clue to his identity behind in the shape of a cigarette-roller bear-

[1] In his book, *The Dead Sea Scrolls* (1955), p. 16. This book is the fullest and most authoritative popular account of the scrolls that has appeared thus far.

ing his name; Mr. Harding was able later on to give it back to him and tell him where he had left it. It was probably as a result of the illegal excavation that the Syrian monastery acquired three fragments of the Book of Daniel from two separate scrolls; one of these fragments contains the passage in Dan. 2:4 where the Hebrew text of the book gives way to Aramaic.

The expert excavation of the cave was carried on with the utmost care; in consequence, several hundred fragments of inscribed leather and a few papyrus fragments were discovered. Most of these fragments were so small and brittle that the excavation had to be done with penknives, tweezers, small brushes and fingers; otherwise irreparable damage would have been done. No intact jars were found, but there was an abundance of broken sherds, and also several pieces of the linen in which the scrolls had been wrapped before being put into the jars.

The use of jars to keep scrolls in was natural and widespread in antiquity. There are early Egyptian examples of this practice, and the Old Testament records how the prophet Jeremiah, on the eve of the Babylonian exile, deposited the purchase-deeds of a field near Jerusalem in an earthenware vessel, so that they might be preserved safely until the people returned from captivity (Jer. 32: 14). A first-century Jewish work entitled *The Assumption of Moses* tells how Moses handed his writings to Joshua with instructions to steep them in cedar oil and place them in earthenware jars. (The cedar oil was calculated to preserve the skin or leather on which the words were written; it is possible that some of the Qumran scrolls were treated in this way before being wrapped in leather.)

The fragments recovered from the cave included portions of other Biblical books in Hebrew—Genesis, Exodus, Leviticus, Deuteronomy, Judges, Samuel, Isaiah, Ezekiel, and the Psalms. The fragments of Isaiah proved to belong to the imperfect scroll of that book which the Hebrew University secured in November, 1947. The fragments of Deuteronomy were written in an archaic script—the "Phoenician" or Palaeo-Hebrew character in which Hebrew was written in earlier days, before the "square" letters which we now associate with Hebrew came into use for the writing of that language. Previously the square letters were used in writing Aramaic, but towards the end of the third century B.C. they came to be used for writing Hebrew too, displacing the older

Phoenician characters. Does this mean that the Leviticus fragments belong to a manuscript written at a time when the Phoenician script was in common use for writing Hebrew? Some have thought so; one scholar would date it as far back as 450 B.C. But in the case of this manuscript we are possibly dealing with a standardized professional literary script which continued to be used for two or three centuries without much change. Even so, these Leviticus fragments have claims to be regarded as older than any of the other documents found in the cave.

There were also fragments of non-Biblical works—commentaries on Micah, Zephaniah and the Psalms; apocryphal works like the *Book of Jubilees*, the *Book of Noah*, and the *Testament of Levi*; works dealing with the life and worship of a religious community; collections of hymns, and so forth.

As the news of these discoveries spread, the excitement of scholars increased, and a bewildering variety of views were ventilated on the date, origin, meaning and purpose of the scrolls. The actual discovery and publication of the documents reflected a high degree of co-operation between Muslims, Jews and Christians of varying traditions at a time when racial and religious animosities were burning fiercely in Palestine and the surrounding territories. Professor Sukenik, for example, made public acknowledgment of his gratitude to Christians and Muslims of Bethlehem for the aid which he, a Jewish scholar, received from them in securing the scrolls which he purchased for the Hebrew University in the later part of 1947. Unfortunately, a similar degree of friendly co-operation (or at least mutual tolerance) was not always evident on the part of some scholars who engaged in what has been called "The Battle of the Scrolls." However, the dust of that battle has largely cleared away. As more and more discoveries have been made, and their results published, the main outlines at least of the answers to questions about the date and provenance of the manuscripts have become increasingly discernible.

Other Caves

For some time it was taken for granted that the cave in which all these discoveries were made was the only cave of its kind in the area. But the local Bedouin were more optimistic. The original finders of the manuscripts had not realized the importance which the world of scholarship would attach to their discoveries. But now their fellow-tribesmen in their simplicity argued that if manuscripts were found in one cave, there might be further manuscripts awaiting discovery in other caves with which the sides of the Wadi Qumran and neighbouring water-courses were honeycombed. So they began to explore the area thoroughly, and in several caves their diligence was rewarded. News got around that further scrolls were available for purchase, and the prices now being charged by the finders were considerably stiffer than those which Muhammad adh-Dhib and his comrades had received for the original lot. To be sure, this private enterprise was illegal, for antiquities ought to be handed over to the government authorities. But in the case of such fragile antiquities as these, the finders must be treated diplomatically, lest the precious documents should be sold to dealers or tourists and dispersed, or otherwise lost or destroyed through careless handling or exposure to damp. Learned institutions throughout the world were invited to co-operate in the acquisition of the manuscripts. Where the archaeological authorities of Jordan got on the track of fresh discoveries, they enlisted the goodwill and co-operative help of the Bedouin who had forestalled them; and by such means further caves were explored and more finds were made. About ten caves in all in the Wadi Qumran yielded treasure of this kind. These caves are conveniently designated by numbers. The cave where the original discoveries were made is naturally known as Cave 1—more concisely, 1Q, where Q stands for Qumran—and the others are numbered Cave 2, Cave 3, and so on.

In Cave 3 a unique discovery was made—inscribed rolls not of skin or papyrus but of copper. There were two rolls, but one of them consisted of two strips of copper rolled up together. It looked as if they were originally riveted end to end to form a sheet of metal about eight feet long by one foot high. It was plain from the outside that they contained writing, but what the writing had to say was not easy to determine. The rolls could not be unrolled because the copper was completely oxidized. At last, early in 1956, they yielded to expert treatment in the Manchester College of Technology, under the direction of Professor

H. Wright Baker of the Chair of Mechanical Engineering. A spindle was put through the rolls; the rolls were coated with glue, baked hard in an oven, and cut into strips with a tiny circular saw. Each strip was photographed as it was cut, and dust and débris were removed from the remaining part, stage by stage, by vacuum suction and a dental brush.

The text thus revealed consisted of about 3,000 letters, and so carefully and skilfully had the operation been carried out that not more than five per cent of the text was destroyed, and of the rest only about two per cent was illegible.

Simultaneous announcements of the contents of these scrolls were made on May 31, 1956, in Manchester and Amman. They contained a collection of traditions about the hiding-places of some sixty hoards of treasure—gold, silver, incense and the like. This treasure, according to the inscription, had been deposited in hiding-places as far distant as Mount Gerizim and Hebron (nearly fifty miles apart), but most of the hiding-places were in the vicinity of Jerusalem. The exact localities indicated would be difficult to identify at this time of day; three samples of the directions were quoted in the first announcement, as follows:

> . . . In the cistern which is below the rampart, on the east side, in a place hollowed out of rock: six hundred bars of silver . . .
> . . . Close by, below the southern corner of the portico at Zadok's tomb,[1] and underneath the pilaster in the exedras, a vessel of incense in pine wood and a vessel of incense in cassia wood . . .
> . . . In the pit near by towards the north, near the graves, in a hole opening to the north, there is a copy of this book, with explanations, measurements and all details . . .

All the material for the perfect treasure hunt, especially if the second copy of the document is located! The gold and silver listed, we are told, amount to nearly 200 tons' weight; and some of the hoards were buried 16 to 18 feet underground. Too bad if the Romans or some other early adventurers lighted upon this treasure trove first; worse still, if some godly Essene simply wrote out the directions by way of a practical joke on posterity![2]

[1] An interesting reference, when we consider that the people who owned the scrolls called themselves the sons of Zadok.

[2] One view is that the document is a compilation of traditions (possibly legendary) concerning buried treasure.

The lettering, it is said, was hastily punched out (with about ten punching blows to a letter), and the scrolls were rolled up hurriedly by unskilled hands. The language is what is known as colloquial Mishnaic (post-Biblical) Hebrew; this is the earliest known text in this kind of Hebrew.

This disposes of the widely held theory that the copper scrolls contained a set of rules and regulations nailed to the wall of the community headquarters. But it must also be pointed out that the announcement in some degree confirms the view earlier expressed by Professor K. G. Kuhn of Göttingen University, who in 1953 examined as much of the writing as was decipherable in reverse on the outside of the copper scrolls, and concluded that they contained a record of the community's treasures and the places where they were hidden when the headquarters were abandoned.[1]

Among all these caves the one which yielded the greatest abundance of literary treasure was Cave 4. Tens of thousands of manuscript fragments were recovered from this cave. These fragments had once constituted about 330 separate books. Ninety of these books were parts of the Bible. Every Old Testament book except Esther is represented among them; some Old Testament books are represented several times over. From all the Qumran caves over 400 separate books have been identified, a few of them being almost intact, but the great majority surviving only in fragments.

In addition to books of the Bible, the discoveries include apocryphal works, such as the Hebrew and Aramaic fragments of the *Book of Tobit* discovered in Cave 5; uncanonical works, such as the *Book of Jubilees*, the *Book of Enoch*, the *Testament of Levi*, and so forth; several works hitherto unknown, such as a description of the New Jerusalem; commentaries and paraphrases, collections of hymns, and documents with a bearing on the beliefs and practices of some religious community. It was a reasonable working hypothesis that this might have been the community to which the books originally belonged, and that some at least of the rest of the literature discovered might provide a clue to the special interests of that community. The *Rule of the Community* found in Cave 1, and represented also by fragments

[1] *Cf.* his article, "Les Rouleaux de Cuivre de Qumran," in *Revue Biblique* 61 (1954), pp. 193 ff.

found in Cave 4, appeared to offer specially full information about the ideals and organization of the community. It was not long before affinities were detected between it and another ancient Jewish work which was discovered some fifty years before. This work, extant in two fragmentary manuscripts written between the tenth and the twelfth centuries A.D., was found in the genizah of the synagogue in Old Cairo, along with many other documents of comparable date. It seems, however, to comprise two treatises—an *Admonition* and a selection of *Laws*—produced about the beginning of the Christian era within a Jewish community which cherished the priestly traditions of the sons of Zadok. For this reason it is frequently described as the Zadokite work,[1] and the community in which it was produced has been called the community of the Zadokites, or (from other references in the fragments) the New Covenanters. It was therefore specially significant that further fragments of the Zadokite work turned up in the Qumran caves. Further study has led to the conclusion that the community referred to in the Zadokite fragments was identical with that described in the *Rule of the Community*.

All these fragments from the caves have to be subjected to a lengthy and delicate process of cleaning, unfolding, smoothing out, and placing between glass. Infra-red photography brings to light writing which the naked eye can no longer discern. The task of piecing together the fragments which originally belonged to one and the same book is not an easy one. It is least difficult where the book is already well known (a book of the Bible, for example); but where the book in question has been completely unknown hitherto, the task is not an enviable one. It is worse than trying to reconstruct a jigsaw puzzle when most of the pieces have disappeared and pieces from other jigsaws have become mixed up with the pieces that remain.

An international team of eight scholars is engaged on this tedious but fascinating work in the Palestine Archaeological Museum, in a long room set apart for this purpose, which is familiarly known as the "Scrollery." A full report of all the fragments recovered from Cave 1 (apart from the seven major documents found in 1947) has been published in the first volume of a series entitled

[1] It is also frequently called the Damascus document, from its references to a period of exile in the land of Damascus. See p. 108.

Discoveries in the Judaean Desert, edited by Fathers D. Barthélemy and J. T. Milik (Clarendon Press, Oxford, 1955). Other volumes (ten or more) will follow as soon as the various bodies of material are ready for publication.

CHAPTER III

DATING THE FINDS

FROM the earliest announcement of the discoveries there has been much disputation about the date of the manuscripts. It is not a bad thing that this has been so. It would be a thousand pities, when the issues at stake are so important, if the pronouncements of even the most eminent and competent scholars were accepted without question. Fortunately, in these fields of study (as in others), scholars are rarely disposed to accept one another's dicta, especially when these dicta are so revolutionary in substance and in implication.

But in the ardour of debate there has at times been a tendency to confuse questions that should be kept distinct. When we talk about the date of the scrolls, we should realize that at least three separate questions are involved:

1. *When were the works represented by the various manuscripts originally written?*
2. *When were the manuscripts themselves copied?*
3. *When were the manuscripts deposited in the caves?*

The first and second questions coincide only when we are dealing with an autograph, the manuscript actually written by the author himself or by someone else at his dictation. For example, if (by a long stretch of the imagination) we were to light one day upon the actual draft of the prophet Isaiah's earlier oracles which he sealed up and handed to his disciples for safe keeping, according to Isa. 8: 16, the date of the manuscript would be identical with the date of the original draft—734 B.C. But, in point of fact, we have no manuscript of any of Isaiah's prophecies anything like so old as that. The earliest manuscript of his prophecies that we know of is the complete scroll of the Book of Isaiah found in Cave 1 at Qumran, and if it is to be dated (as seems probable) in the second century B.C., then nearly six hundred years separate it from the original draft which Isaiah wrote or dictated. In the actual state of affairs, the answers to Questions 1 and 2 are quite distinct.

1. *When were the works represented by the various manuscripts originally written?*

This is a question which must be answered firstly by a careful study of the contents of each work (that is to say, by internal evidence), and secondly by considering any allusions which may be made to the work in question in other documents which can be dated independently (that is to say, by external evidence). This is the line of approach which used to be known as "higher criticism"—a branch of study which is by no means confined to Biblical literature.

As concerns the Biblical writings found at Qumran, we have already ample internal and external evidence for coming to conclusions about their date and authorship. The new discoveries add scarcely anything to our knowledge in this respect. But our evidence is much scantier for many of the non-Biblical works which have come to light.

A good example of the position is provided by a manuscript which combines a Biblical text with something else. The commentary on the Book of Habakkuk discovered in Cave 1 contains the Hebrew text of part of that book together with a commentary on the text. Obviously the Hebrew text of Habakkuk must be earlier in date than the commentary appended to it. The internal and external evidence for the date of the one will be quite different from the evidence for the date of the other.

The Book of Habakkuk as we have it now consists of two compositions. One of these, contained in Chapters 1 and 2, is entitled "The oracle of God which Habakkuk the prophet saw"; the other, contained in Chapter 3, is entitled "A prayer of Habakkuk the prophet, according to Shigionoth," and is actually a psalm, complete in itself. The Qumran manuscript has the text of the first two chapters only, with a running commentary, and it is plain from the state of the manuscript that it never contained the text of the third chapter. Probably the *Oracle of Habakkuk* and the *Psalm of Habakkuk* were regarded as two quite distinct works.

The internal evidence of the first two chapters of Habakkuk

suggests that they were composed somewhere in the land of Judah around the year 600 B.C. The author laments the oppression which he sees on every hand, and wonders why God does not intervene to defend the right against the rulers of his nation who pervert justice. He is told that a judgment is about to befall these unrighteous rulers; the Chaldaeans will invade the land and sweep them from their misused eminence. Later, the prophet complains that the Chaldaeans are even more oppressive than the Jewish rulers who fell before them, and he receives further assurances that God will accomplish His purpose and vindicate His righteousness in His own good time. Since we know that the Chaldaeans became a power to be reckoned with in Judah and the neighbouring lands in 605 B.C., and that they occupied Jerusalem in 597 B.C. and destroyed it in 587 B.C., it is easy to conclude that the various parts of the first two chapters of Habakkuk are to be dated in the course of these years. The title of these two chapters—"The oracle of God which Habakkuk the prophet saw"—gives the prophet's name.

As regards external evidence, the earliest we have is a statement in the Septuagint, prefaced to the legend of Bel and the Dragon (one of the apocryphal additions to Daniel), which mentions Habakkuk's prophecy and describes him as "Habakkuk the son of Joshua of the tribe of Levi." The tradition that he was a Levite may be true, but the part which he plays in the story of Bel and the Dragon is as unhistorical as the rest of the story. All that this external evidence indicates, then, is that about 100 B.C. (the approximate date of the Greek version of Bel and the Dragon) Habakkuk the prophet and his prophecy were well known and were believed to belong to the period of the Babylonian exile.

Of course the internal and external evidence for the date of the prophecy of Habakkuk has no direct bearing on the Dead Sea Scrolls; it has been discussed here merely to illustrate how such evidence is recognized and used. What does directly concern us is the evidence for the running commentary attached to the text of Habakkuk's prophecy in the manuscript which we are considering.

This commentary is in itself "external" evidence for the existence of Habakkuk's prophecy at the time when the commentary was written; it also shows clearly that at that time

Habakkuk's prophecy was venerated as holy writ. But how are we to decide the time at which the commentary was written? If we can determine the date at which the scrolls were deposited in Qumran Cave 1, and if, further, we can determine the date at which this particular scroll was copied out, we shall know that the composition of the commentary cannot be later than these dates. Thus far there does not seem to be any more direct external evidence that would enable us to date the composition of the commentary. But internal evidence should in any case be considered first. What does the internal evidence for the commentary amount to?

One thing is plain; the commentator believes that the prophecy which he is concerned to interpret is being fulfilled in his own day, and he describes persons and events of his own day so as to show that Habakkuk was really foretelling *them*. Unfortunately for us, he describes those contemporary persons and events in such an allusive style that scholars are not yet in agreement about their identity. Can we identify them with persons and events already known in history?

Habakkuk had spoken of the rise of the Chaldaeans and their conquering advance—things which took place in his own lifetime. But the commentator does not think that Habakkuk really meant to speak of the Chaldaeans and their empire; in actual fact, he maintains, Habakkuk was describing in advance imperial conquerors of the commentator's day. Habakkuk *said* the "Chaldaeans" but he really *meant* the "Kitti'im"—people who, at the time when the commentator was writing, had come from across the sea and were imposing their yoke on all lands. The question then is: Who were these "Kitti'im"—the people of "Kittim"? Originally the term Kittim denoted Cyprus (or even more particularly the Phoenician settlements around Kition, the modern Larnaka); but it came more generally to mean the Greek islands and coastlands of the Eastern Mediterranean. In the Book of Daniel it is used of the Romans (Dan. 11: 30), possibly because the incident referred to there was regarded as the fulfilment of an ancient oracle of Balaam in which ships from Kittim are mentioned (Num. 24: 24).

If an imperial conqueror from the Mediterranean lands is sought to satisfy the commentator's description of the Kitti'im, then we may think either of Alexander the Great and his successors or of the Romans. The suggestion of one scholar that they are to be identified with the Crusaders of the eleventh and twelfth centuries A.D., is really put out of court by the contents of the commentary, as well as by all that we can discover about the age of the manuscript and the time at which it was deposited along with its companions in the cave.

If we consider Alexander and his successors to be denoted by the Kitti'im, then the reference will probably be more particularly to Antiochus IV (175–163 B.C.), whose attempt to suppress the ancestral religion and customs of the Jewish nation led to the patriotic rising under Judas Maccabaeus and his family, of which we may read in the Books of Maccabees.[1] But some reasons will be suggested later[2] for thinking that the commentary reflects the conditions of the following century, and that the Kitti'im are the Romans; the commentary in that case would be written shortly before the occupation of Judæa and Jerusalem by the Roman general Pompey in 63 B.C.

2. *When were the manuscripts themselves copied?*

There is one branch of study which is more helpful than most in this matter of determining when a particular manuscript was written. This is the study known as palaeography—the study of ancient handwriting. We know how in more recent times the style of handwriting tends to vary in our own country from generation to generation. Our grandfathers used a different style of handwriting from ours—and one, it must be added, which was much more legible and pleasing to look at. So too in more remote times styles of handwriting varied from one generation to another and from one country to another. This means that the date of a manuscript can be determined, within reasonable limits, by the characteristics of the writing which it exhibits. Greek and Latin palaeography has been studied for such a long time, and has such an abundance of material to work upon, that it has become almost an exact science. Classical palaeographers usually find themselves in general agreement about the dating of Greek and Latin

[1] The ablest statement and defence of this identification of the Kitti'im is given by Professor H. H. Rowley in *The Zadokite Fragments and the Dead Sea Scrolls* (1952).

[2] See pp. 72 ff., 138.

manuscripts from the closing centuries B.C. down to the invention of printing in the fifteenth century A.D. and later still.

Hebrew and Aramaic palaeography is at a disadvantage as compared with Greek and Latin palaeography in that it has not nearly so much material to work upon so far as the pre-Christian era and the earlier centuries A.D. are concerned. None the less it is as exact a science in principle as any other branch of palaeography. And it is worthy of note that the scholars who have examined the Dead Sea manuscripts on the basis of palaeography have for the most part agreed upon an early date for them—that is to say, a date in the closing centuries B.C. or the early years A.D. The scholars who have argued for a considerably later date are not palaeographers; some of them, indeed, have gone so far as to dismiss the palaeographical evidence as worthless—an odd example of obscurantism from an unwonted quarter!

It was the palaeographical evidence that from the outset convinced Sukenik and Albright of the antiquity of the scrolls, and the palaeographical evidence still supplies the main proof of their antiquity, although there is, as we shall see, further corroborative evidence of other kinds.

In fact, the palaeographical evidence can be dismissed only if it is shown that the scrolls are fabrications of a later age, deliberately written in an archaic script so as to deceive readers, and planted in order to be "discovered," like the Piltdown skull, at an opportune moment. There have been fakes of this sort in the past. But they have been detected and exposed very quickly, as soon as they were submitted to competent judges, like Clermont-Ganneau, who exposed the Shapira fraud, or Tischendorf, who exposed the Simonides forgeries.[1] But never have ancient manuscripts been viewed with greater scepticism, or subjected to more rigorous examination, than these Qumran documents. All the circumstances of their finding rule out the possibility of deliberate fraud; the Bedouin who have been demanding such inflated prices for their discoveries are not the sort of people who could manufacture the fragments which are proving such a windfall to them; and university libraries and other learned foundations are not likely to pay large sums of money for their acquisition without being satisfied of their value. Dr. H. J. Plenderleith, Keeper of

[1] Constantine Simonides, a hundred years ago, produced a number of fakes, including several allegedly first-century fragments of the New Testament.

the Research Laboratory at the British Museum, speaking of some fragments from Cave 1 which had been submitted to him for special treatment, said that "twenty-five years of experience in the handling of antiquities had convinced him at once that the materials were genuine, a conviction which was, subsequently, fully justified when the fragments were submitted to scientific examination."[1]

Among Semitic palaeographers in Great Britain, Dr. S. A. Birnbaum, of the London School of Oriental and African Studies, occupies a position second to none. He is at present publishing the material on which the science of Hebrew palaeography is based in a great work entitled *The Hebrew Scripts*. His verdict on the date of the first published scrolls was given in a valuable little study on *The Qumrân (Dead Sea) Scrolls and Palaeography* (1952); the Habakkuk scroll, he held, was copied between 100 and 50 B.C.; the *Rule of the Community* between 125 and 100 B.C., and the complete Isaiah scroll (Isaiah A) between 175 and 150 B.C. The Isaiah scroll's greater antiquity than its companions is further attested by signs of wear and tear; it had clearly been used for quite a long time before it was deposited with the others in the cave. Dr. J. C. Trever, who accepts Dr. Birnbaum's relative dating of these scrolls, would date each of them a few decades later—Isaiah A between 125 and 100 B.C., the scroll of the *Rule* about 75 B.C., the Habakkuk scroll (and the fourth scroll acquired by the Syrian monastery) between 25 B.C. and A.D. 25.

The more recent tendency appears to favour these lower dates rather than the higher ones suggested by Dr. Birnbaum. But the abundance of manuscript material provided by the caves explored from 1952 onwards has advanced the study of Hebrew palaeography beyond all expectation. A clear distinction can now be made between the development of the more formal book-hand and the less formal cursive script used for everyday purposes. The book-hand was used by preference for Biblical manuscripts; the cursive was used commonly for community documents and Aramaic works. All stages of the evolution of these two hands are represented in the Qumran caves from the third century B.C. to the first century A.D. The older Phoenician (Palaeo-Hebrew) script also appears to have survived in use for certain purposes longer than was formerly realized, and to have been employed side by side with the book-hand and cursive forms of the square script.

[1] *Journal of Transactions of the Victoria Institute* 82 (1950), p. 146.

Further evidence of a rather later stage in the evolution of the square script has been forthcoming from another important manuscript find in the Wadi Murabba'at, about twelve miles south of the Wadi Qumran, of which more will be said in a later chapter; some of these latter documents, unlike those at Qumran, bear explicit dates (in the second century A.D.) and thus supply a reliable criterion for fixing the chronology of other stages in the evolution.

Questions have been asked about the composition of the ink and the ruling of the scrolls with guiding lines (horizontally, to keep the lines of writing straight, and vertically, to keep the edges of the columns straight). Does a study of these things throw any light on the date of the manuscripts?

In a letter to *The Times* of September 22, 1949, Professor G. R. Driver suggested that an analysis of the ink might provide information about their date. Was it a metallic ink or not? "If it is metallic, they are likely to be later than the Mishnah (*c.* A.D. 200);[1] but, if it is non-metallic, they may be earlier, even though in this case the test will be inconclusive, as non-metallic ink may have continued in use beside metallic ink for many centuries." The analysis, when it was carried out, was quite conclusive in a chemical sense. No metal was present in the ink; carbon alone was used. But this simply meant, as Dr. Plenderleith pointed out, "that the nature of the ink cannot be regarded as vital evidence for dating purposes."[2] It does not exclude the dating assigned to the scrolls by the paleographers.

Nor does the ruling of the writing material give us any more positive indication. The use of guiding lines to keep the writing straight is of quite considerable antiquity. Ruled papyri have been found belonging to the first century A.D. and even earlier. And if it was found necessary to rule papyrus, the fibres of which are usually sufficiently straight and parallel to serve as natural guiding lines, how much more necessary must it have been to rule the smooth surface of a skin which was prepared to receive writing!

The composition of the ink and the nature of the ruling, it appears, neither confirm nor contradict the palaeographical findings.

[1] But Dr. Birnbaum says there was iron in the ink used for the Lachish Letters in 588 B.C.!

[2] *Journal of Transactions of the Victoria Institute* 82 (1950), p. 146.

The palaeographical findings point fairly definitely to the last two or three centuries of the Second Jewish Commonwealth (the period ending A.D. 70) as the time within which the manuscripts were copied.

3. *When were the manuscripts deposited in the caves?*

It looks very much as if the manuscripts found in the Qumran caves represent a large library which was moved from its usual headquarters because of the approach of some danger. But this likelihood does not help us very much in our endeavour to decide *when* the library was moved, because history knows of so many dangerous situations in that part of the world. "Palestine has had a long and troubled history," says Professor Driver, "and the fugitives who hid these Scrolls in the cave near Jericho might be fleeing not from the persecution which Antiochus Epiphanes set in motion (165 B.C.) nor from the invasions of the Romans (63 B.C., A.D. 70 and 135) nor even from those of the Persians (A.D. 614) or of the Arabs (A.D. 637) but perhaps merely from some local tumult caused by racial or religious hatred of which history has preserved no record."[1]

But there are certain lines of evidence which enable us to choose to some degree among these diverse possibilities. When the scrolls were deposited, they were wrapped in linen and placed in earthenware jars. Can any conclusion be reached by an examination of the linen and the earthenware?

First, the linen. Very recently a new method of dating organic material from its radiocarbon content—a method known as the "Carbon 14" method—has been devised. This method, still in its experimental stage, is used to determine how long ago an organic substance ceased to "live." A simple account of the principle involved is given by Sir Mortimer Wheeler in his Pelican book *Archaeology from the Earth* (1956), pp. 50 ff. Linen is, of course, an organic material, and the application of the Carbon 14 method to a piece of linen would aim at showing the approximate date at which the flax was cut. In 1950 four ounces of the linen in which the scrolls were wrapped were tested by this new technique in the Institute for Nuclear Studies of Chicago University. On January 9, 1951, Professor W. F. Libby, who had conducted the test, reported that it yielded A.D. 33, with a margin of 200 years

[1] *The Hebrew Scrolls*, p. 50. The cave referred to is Cave 1.

before and after, as the date when the organism died—i.e. when the flax from which the linen was made ceased to grow. Naturally, the linen would be manufactured soon after the flax was cut. The linen need not have been quite new when the scrolls were wrapped in it, but it would not have been extremely old. The scrolls, moreover, may have been kept in these linen wrappings before they were deposited in the caves. But the results of the Carbon 14 test, for what they are worth, fit quite well into the general picture which is gradually being built up on the basis of other kinds of evidence.

What of the jars found in the caves? Earthenware articles intended for use and not for ornament did not have a longer life in antiquity than they do in our day. If, therefore, the scrolls were placed in the jars at the time when they were deposited in the caves, we should not expect the age of the jars to go back very much earlier than the date of the deposit. The value of pottery for establishing chronology has been increasingly recognized over the past seventy years, the first archaeologist to appreciate its significance properly being Sir Flinders Petrie. Styles of pottery change with surprising suddenness at irregular intervals, but within these intervals they tend to persist with little variation over a remarkably wide area. And as earthenware pots are by far the commonest articles made by human hands, layers of human occupation on ancient sites can be dated with reasonable accuracy by a study of the immense quantities of potsherds found in successive layers. In default of expressly dated inscriptions there are few criteria which can be so confidently used for archaeological dating as the pottery criterion. The jars found with the Qumran manuscripts are of an unusual type; no wonder, for it appears from their shape that they were specially manufactured to contain the scrolls. They are cylindrical in form, about two feet high and ten inches in diameter, and were provided with inverted bowls to serve as lids. In some cases the decomposition of the edge of a scroll near the opening of its jar formed a pitch-like substance which effectively sealed the jar; this explains why a few scrolls, in unbroken jars, were preserved in such good condition while the majority slowly disintegrated throughout the centuries because of exposure to air and moisture and the attentions of various small animals.

But if the type of the jars in the caves could not be paralleled from ordinary domestic ware, the texture of the pottery proved to be characteristic of the early Roman period.

The remains of earthenware lamps found in Cave 1 represent types known to be characteristic in part of the late Hellenistic period and in part of the Roman period.

A more definite result, however, is provided by a jar of exactly the same type as those used to accommodate the scrolls, which was discovered on a site near the caves in association with other objects which could be dated with absolute precision. This site was the headquarters of the community to which the manuscripts belonged, and to it we must now turn our attention.

CHAPTER IV

KHIRBET QUMRAN

ON a rocky shelf on the north side of the Wadi Qumran, nearly three-quarters of a mile west of the Dead Sea, lie ruins which have long been known by the name Khirbet Qumran.[1] In 1873 the French archaeologist Clermont-Ganneau, whose name has already been mentioned in connexion with the exposure of the Shapira forgery, paid some attention to these ruins, although he was more interested in an ancient cemetery which lies between them and the Dead Sea. But he came to no definite conclusion as a result of his investigations.

When the first official archaeological party visited Cave 1 in 1949, they wondered if there might be any connexion between the discoveries in the cave and the ruined site of Khirbet Qumran. A trial excavation was made on the site, but nothing was found which suggested any connexion. In November and December, 1951, however, three rooms of the ruined building were excavated. In the floor of one of these rooms a jar was found of exactly the same type as those found in Cave 1, and along with it was a coin dated A.D. 10! Obviously there was more connexion between Khirbet Qumran and the manuscript deposit than they had thought; further exploration of the site must be undertaken. Accordingly systematic campaigns of excavation have been carried out in the spring of 1953, 1954 and 1955. The Jordanian Department of Antiquities, the Dominican *École Biblique* and the Palestine Archaeological Museum have co-operated in this enterprise.

It soon became evident that the building formed the headquarters of a large and well-organized community. Not long after the systematic excavation of the site began, Father de Vaux expressed his belief that they had located the headquarters of the Jewish sect of the Essenes referred to by the first-century Roman

[1] Tentatively identified with "the City of Salt" mentioned in Joshua 15: 61.

writer Pliny the Elder. For Pliny said that these people lived on the west shore of the Dead Sea, above En-gedi (which actually lies some twenty miles south of Khirbet Qumran).

It is with the community which occupied the building that the cemetery which lies to the east of it is most probably to be associated. We know of no other occupation which could have given rise to so many burials of such a uniform pattern. There are over a thousand burials, laid out in parallel rows lying north and south, with the head to the south (only one exception has been noted to this rule).[1] The burials were as simple as could be; the bodies were not accompanied by funeral offerings, nor even placed in coffins. Each was laid face upwards in a small mortuary chamber at the bottom of a trench. The entrance to the mortuary chamber was then walled up with a layer of unbaked brick or a stone slab; the trench was filled in, and the burial was marked on the surface by two upright stones with a row of pebbles between them. A few potsherds in the earth filling of the graves point to the period during which the neighbouring ruins were occupied by the community. Skeletons of women as well as men were found in the cemetery. This fact, together with some others of a different kind which will be mentioned in due course, suggests that, if we are indeed dealing with the remains of an Essene community, it must have belonged to that exceptional group of Essenes mentioned by Josephus as practising matrimony, as distinct from all the other Essenes, who were devoted to celibacy.

Researches on the site of Khirbet Qumran show that it was occupied at various times in antiquity. At a low level the remains of walls and pottery were found which belonged to the period known to archaeologists as Iron Age II (the eighth and seventh centuries B.C.). One of the potsherds found at this level was inscribed with Phoenician characters of the kind used for writing Hebrew at that time. One suggestion is that this building, from the period of the Hebrew monarchy, illustrates a statement made about King Uzziah of Judah (*c.* 780–740 B.C.) in II Chron. 26: 10, that "he built towers in the wilderness."

At the other end of the record there is evidence of brief and sporadic occupation of the site in the Arab period.

But chief interest attaches to the abundant evidence of the

[1] Muslim burials are orientated east and west. See p. 138.

occupation of the site in the Graeco-Roman period. Three quite separate stages of occupation can be distinguished in this period:

1. Occupation by a religious community from the end of the second century B.C. to A.D. 68.
2. Occupation by a Roman garrison between A.D. 68 and 86.
3. Occupation by Jewish insurgents in the second war against Rome, A.D. 132–135.

The first of these stages is itself divided into two parts. The community appears to have left the building for between thirty and forty years at the end of the first century B.C.; and not long after they left it it was severely damaged by an earthquake, so that extensive reconstruction was necessary when they returned to occupy it again.

The main building occupied by the community as its headquarters was roughly 120 feet square, constructed of large undressed stones, with a strong tower at the north-west corner. There were several large rooms, suitable for assembly-rooms or refectories. The largest room thus far excavated, on the south of the main building, seems to have served as the main refectory; adjoining it was a smaller room containing about 1,700 earthenware vessels—all the varieties necessary for kitchen and dining-room use. These vessels were probably made on the premises, for the excavations have revealed the best-preserved pottery factory thus far known from ancient Palestine. It is well within the bounds of probability that the jars which accommodated the scrolls were manufactured here too.

And not only the jars, but some of the scrolls which they contained, may well have been produced in this building. For a first-storey room in the south-west part of the building was evidently furnished as a writing-room or *scriptorium*. It contained a long table of plaster, moulded on a brick framework, suitable for use as a writing-table. That it was actually so used seems confirmed by the discovery in the same place of two inkwells, one earthenware, and one bronze. One of these had the dried remains of carbon ink still adhering to its inner surface. Two plaster hand-basins found along with them have been explained as basins where the scribes might perform the ritual washing of their hands which was called for when the name of God had to be written.

When this explanation of the room as a scriptorium was given in a broadcast talk by Professor H. H. Rowley towards the end of 1954, one scholar wrote to *The Listener* protesting that it was physically impossible to write at the table in question, which was (he maintained) intended to be used for Christian love-feasts. Another scholar wrote to point out that this writer had overlooked the two inkwells found in the *scriptorium*. "But perhaps," he added, "he regards these as chalices." The answer which this remark called forth belongs to the realm of oral tradition, and must remain there!

No manuscripts have been discovered in the building hitherto, apart from a practice copy of the Hebrew alphabet belonging to the earlier phase of its occupation by the community.

Flour mills, storage bins, ovens, smelting furnaces and workshops with metal implements are among the other installations laid bare on the site. Evidently the community which was centred on this place aimed at being as self-contained as possible. One of the most striking features of the whole area was the elaborately organized water-supply. Water was brought from the hills to the north-west in a carefully constructed channel which ran west and south of the building and emptied itself into a number of cisterns. Quite plainly the water was not required solely for the ordinary purposes of washing and drinking; the presence of several swimming-pools or baptisteries suggested that it was required for ritual purification and indicated that the community was one of a number of baptist sects which we know to have flourished in the Jordan valley and neighbourhood in the years before and after the commencement of the Christian era. The most elaborate of these baptisteries had fourteen stone steps leading down into it. These steps show a central crack running all the way down from top to bottom, so that their eastern half has sunk about a foot and a half below the level of the western half. This crack was a result of the earthquake which damaged the rest of the building. When the community, which was not in residence at the time when the earthquake occurred, resumed occupation of the site several years later, this baptistery could no longer be used (it could not now retain water, and the damage was too extensive to be easily repaired); a new baptistery was constructed south of the building. Other major repairs had to be undertaken at the same time; the north-western tower was reinforced and the walls were generally strengthened. But the general ground-plan was preserved and the building obviously continued to serve the same purposes as before.

The earthquake which caused this damage has been identified, quite convincingly, with one which Josephus describes as having devastated Judæa in 31 B.C., the seventh year of the reign of Herod the Great, who was engaged in a war with his Arabian neighbours across the Jordan at the time.

We have said that when a beginning was made with the excavation of the site in 1951, a coin of A.D. 10 was found in close conjunction with a jar of identical type to those found in the caves. Later excavation has brought to light several hundred coins of the Graeco-Roman period, by which the successive stages of occupation can be dated with reasonable certainty. The record of the coins starts in the reign of John Hyrcanus (135–104 B.C.) and carries us forward without a break to the reign of the last Hasmonean king, Antigonus (40–37 B.C.). But from the long reign of Antigonus's successor, Herod the Great, only one coin has turned up to date. The record is resumed in the reign of Herod's son Archelaus (4 B.C.–A.D. 6), and from then we have a further continuous series of coins taking us on to A.D. 68—six from the reign of Archelaus, three from the Roman procurators of Judæa under the Emperor Augustus (A.D. 6–14), seven of the procurators under Tiberius (A.D. 14–37), a silver coin of Tyre dated A.D. 29, twenty-three coins of Herod Agrippa I (A.D. 37–44), five of the procurators of Judæa under Claudius (A.D. 44–54), fifteen of the procurators under Nero (A.D. 54–66), and eleven struck by Jewish insurgent authorities during the first two years of the first war against Rome (A.D. 66–70). This record comes to an end in A.D. 68.

When we assess the chronological evidence of coins, it is worth reminding ourselves that, while coins are not used before they are struck, they remain in use for many years after they are struck.[1]

[1] A hoard of five hundred and sixty-three coins was discovered in 1955, hidden in three pots in the floor of a room on the west of the building. These were of two kinds: coins of the Seleucid king Antiochus VII (139–129 B.C.) and coins of Tyre (the latest of which was dated 9 B.C.). But these coins were probably hidden in the ruins between 9 and 4 B.C., during the community's absence, and had nothing to do with the community.

The second period of the occupation of Khirbet Qumran by the community was brought to an end neither by a voluntary withdrawal nor by an earthquake, but by the violence of fire and sword. The destruction was much more thorough than that caused by the earthquake nearly a hundred years before. The walls were demolished, a layer of black ash covered the site, and a quantity of arrow-heads added their silent testimony to the general picture.

If Josephus's account of the earthquake of 31 B.C. throws light on the damage wrought at the end of the first period of the building's occupation by the community, another part of his narrative helps to account for the destruction which marked the end of the second period. For he relates that in May of A.D. 68 Vespasian, commander-in-chief of the Roman army in Palestine, came down the Jordan valley to Jericho, and from there the tenth legion advanced against Jerusalem in the following year, leaving a garrison in Jericho. What contacts the community at Qumran may have had with the insurgents we cannot say, but a stronghold like theirs was bound to receive hostile attention from the Roman forces in the district. We can scarcely doubt, then, that it was destroyed by the Romans about this time; and there is no further trace of any connexion between the community and their former headquarters. One further inference which we may safely make from the evidence is that, on the approach of the Romans down the Jordan valley, the members of the community bestowed their literary treasures in the caves which abounded in the vicinity, hoping to retrieve them when the tide of war had receded. But the opportunity for them to retrieve the books never came.

Even after the storming of Jerusalem by the Romans in August of A.D. 70, there were still a few pockets of Jewish resistance left to be mopped up. Of these the one that held out longest was at Masada, on the west shore of the Dead Sea, about twelve miles south of En-gedi. Masada has been excavated quite recently by Israeli archaeologists. One young Englishman who was taken on a sightseeing expedition around those parts by bus in March, 1956, gives the following description:

> We parked at an army camp at the foot of Masada, and set off skywards. Single file was the only possibility, and at places

that was pretty difficult. I was amazed that some quite elderly folk climbed with us. When we reached the top, the chief guide said a few words, and we looked round and rested. They are busy just now excavating Herod's palace. The ruins of a Byzantine church were very interesting, too; but we had all too little time to investigate. We descended by the N.W. route—the one by which the Romans eventually entered; and by the way I must in passing take off my hat to the Romans for even attempting to capture the fortress. The first part of this route was the worst, and it took the hundred and eighty of us two and a half hours to do it; so that the rest of the descent had to be done by the light of one torch and half a moon! At the worst spots soldiers lent a hand, but I was asked to assist at one nasty precipitous bend, so behold me prancing about on a narrow ledge in the moonlight, assuring others that there was nothing to fear. We finally reached the bottom at 9.30 p.m., after which we swathed ourselves in blankets or sleeping-bags, and found the softest rocks we could.

There was thus military activity west of the Dead Sea for some years after the destruction of the community headquarters, and the ruined site suggested itself to the Romans as convenient headquarters for a garrison. A few rooms were therefore built over the ruins, and occupied by a Roman garrison which kept watch over that part of the Dead Sea coast and helped to protect the lines of communication of their comrades who were engaged in the arduous siege of Masada. Nor did they leave the site when Masada was captured; they remained in occupation for ten or twenty years. This military occupation of Khirbet Qumran is represented by a few coins ranging in date from the last two years of Nero's reign to the reign of Titus (A.D. 79–81). A coin of Herod Agrippa II, of date A.D. 86, was found outside the building; it is uncertain whether it should be connected with the Roman military occupation or not.

In A.D. 132 a second Jewish revolt against Rome broke out in Judæa, and was not put down until after three years of bitter and costly guerrilla fighting. We shall have more to say about this second revolt in the following chapter; but it is relevant here because for a short time during this period Khirbet Qumran was occupied by members of the insurgent forces. Fifteen coins bear witness to this brief occupation; they include one coin

L.I.F.E. College Library
1100 Glendale Blvd
Los Angeles, Calif. 90026

of Vespasian (A.D. 69–79), three of Trajan (A.D. 98–117), and one Jewish coin of the type struck by the insurgent leaders during the revolt. This brief occupation was followed by the complete demolition by the Romans of the fortifications of Khirbet Qumran.

CHAPTER V

WADI MURABBA'AT AND KHIRBET MIRD

Wadi Murabba'at

ABOUT the same time as it became known that manuscripts had been found in other caves at Qumran over and above Cave 1, news began to circulate about other manuscript discoveries made in the Wadi Murabba'at, which runs down to the Dead Sea from the west about eleven miles south of the Wadi Qumran and some fifteen miles south-east of Jerusalem. Early in 1952 Bedouin of the same tribe as had discovered the first manuscripts at Qumran were found to be offering for sale pieces of leather with Hebrew and Greek writing on them. The archaeological authorities of Jordan learned that these fragments had come from the Wadi Murabba'at, and when they arrived on the spot with eight Bedouin whom they had brought along to do any necessary digging, they found thirty-four other Bedouin hard at work on their amateur excavations. A number of these were immediately taken into service to carry on the good work under lawful and expert supervision. Four caves in the area contained traces of human occupation at five distinct periods in antiquity—in the Chalcolithic Age (fourth millennium B.C.), the Middle Bronze Age (*c.* 2000–1550 B.C.), the Iron Age (more specifically the eighth and seventh centuries B.C.), the Roman period and the Arab period.

From the third, fourth and fifth of these periods written documents were discovered. From the third period, the era of the later kings of Judah, came two papyrus palimpsests inscribed in Phoenician (Palaeo-Hebrew) letters; the text of both, unfortunately, was wholly secular in substance. From the fifth period came some paper documents in Arabic. But it was from the fourth period, the Roman era, that the most interesting material came.

In A.D. 132, when Hadrian was Roman Emperor, a revolt broke out in Judæa against the Romans. The leader of this revolt was a man named Simeon, who struck coins designating himself as

"Simeon Prince of Israel" and bearing such significant dates as "Year I of the Redemption of Israel"; "Year II of the Freedom of Israel." But his leadership was not purely secular in character; some people believed him to be the long-expected Messiah who would lead Israel to victory against her heathen oppressors. Among those who recognized Simeon as the Messiah was the greatest religious teacher of the day, Rabbi Aqiba. Aqiba hailed Simeon as the conquering hero foretold long ages before by the Mesopotamian prophet Balaam. "A star," said Balaam, "shall come forth out of Jacob"; and he went on to describe how this "star" would crush the enemies of Israel, while Israel under his leadership would perform valiant deeds and exercise dominion (Num. 24: 17–19). Because Aqiba identified Simeon with this predicted "star," Simeon came to be known as Simeon Bar-Kokhba, which is Aramaic for "Simeon son of the Star." There were others who would not acknowledge Simeon's claims (including the Jewish Christians, who naturally could not recognize anyone other than Jesus as the true Messiah); they preferred to call him Simeon Bar-Koziba, which means "Simeon the son of falsehood." Simeon maintained a fierce guerrilla resistance against the Roman forces for over three years, and exacted a heavy toll from them before his revolt was crushed in A.D. 135.

Some of the documents from the Roman era of occupation in the Wadi Murabba'at made it quite clear that Simeon's followers maintained a garrison here, under the command of one Yeshua Ben-Galgolah. Two letters written to Yeshua by Simeon were found, which incidentally showed that Bar-Kokhba and Bar-Koziba were both plays on the wording of Simeon's proper patronymic, which was Ben-Kosebah.[1] That is what he calls himself in these letters. Here is the text of one of them:

> From Simeon Ben-Kosebah to Yeshua Ben-Galgolah and to the men of your company. Peace! I call heaven to witness against me that if one of the Galilaeans whom you have protected troubles us, I will put fetters on your feet as I did to Ben-Aflul. Simeon Ben-Kosebah, Prince of Israel.

Who the luckless Ben-Aflul was, or what he had done, we cannot tell. Nor do we know anything about the Galilaeans mentioned

[1] *Ben* is Hebrew for "son"; *bar* is the corresponding Aramaic word.

in the letter. There is no particular reason to think that they were Jewish Christians. We know that Jewish Christians had to endure considerable persecution at the hands of Simeon and his supporters, because they refused to join his rising, but there is no evidence that they were called Galilaeans. It is safest to suppose that the letter refers to certain troublesome individuals from Galilee of whom no further information is available to us.

There was also a letter addressed to Yeshua by two officials of a Jewish community. Several copies of a legal document in Aramaic are dated "in the third year of the liberation of Israel by the hand of Simeon Ben-Kosebah." Among other dated documents from the second century are some Greek texts on papyrus—a marriage contract dated A.D. 124 (in the seventh year of Hadrian), a contract of reconciliation between a husband and wife, a bond from the year 171, and a document dated in the reign of the Emperor Commodus (A.D. 180–193). There were also some fragments in cursive Latin. This suggests that when the revolt was suppressed, the post was occupied by a Roman garrison for a considerable period.

A few inscribed potsherds (ostraca) were found, most of which bore Hebrew writing, though the writing on some was Greek. Two fragments of Greek literary works were deciphered: one of these was religious in character, the other seemed to deal with the family of Herod, as the names Salome and Mariamne could be distinguished. Could it be a fragment of the work of Nicolas of Damascus, historiographer-royal at the court of Herod the Great? The fragment is too small to lead to any certain conclusion.

But the second-century discoveries on this site included many fragments of Biblical Hebrew manuscripts, written on leather. Among these were fragments of four scrolls—one of Genesis, two of Exodus and one of Deuteronomy—which bore unmistakable signs of having been violently torn up. Was this destruction the work of the Roman soldiers when they stormed the position? It would not have been the first time that Roman soldiery had treated Jewish scripture in this way. Other manuscripts had been reduced to fragments by humbler members of God's creation than Roman soldiers; rats and other small animals had used them to make nests. There was the beginning of a scroll of Isaiah, still showing verses 4 to 14 of Chapter 1. There was a complete phylactery—that is to say, a parchment containing four passages from the Hebrew Bible (Ex. 13: 1–10; Ex. 13: 11–16; Deut. 6: 4–9; Deut. 11: 13–21) in parallel columns, which was placed in a leather container and worn on the forehead or the left arm in literal fulfilment of the divine injunction: "And these words which I command you this day . . . you shall bind them as a sign upon your hand, and they shall be as frontlets between your eyes" (Deut. 6: 6, 8). (Fragmentary phylacteries were found in some of the Qumran caves, but these were of an older type, which included the ten commandments in addition to the passages mentioned above; this type went out of use after A.D. 70.)

From unidentified caves in the neighbourhood of Murabba'at the Bedouin produced another group of manuscripts (mostly fragmentary) very similar in character to those found in the Wadi Murabba'at. Some of them appear to have originated with another insurgent garrison of A.D. 132–135, for they included a Hebrew letter addressed to Simeon Ben-Kosebah and two Aramaic contracts dated "in the third year of the liberation of Israel by the hand of Simeon Ben-Kosebah." There were also two Greek documents and two Aramaic documents dated by the era of the Roman province of Arabia (which was founded by the Emperor Trajan in A.D. 106), and papyrus documents in the Nabataean dialect of Aramaic, longer than any Nabataean documents previously known. Biblical Hebrew texts from this unidentified cache included fragments of Genesis, Numbers, and the Psalms, together with another complete phylactery; there was also a column of a Greek copy of the Book of Habakkuk, which is said to supply an important missing link in the history of the Septuagint. More recently there has come from Murabba'at a scroll of the Minor Prophets in Hebrew, from the middle of Joel to the beginning of Zechariah, belonging to the second century A.D. and closely related to the Massoretic text.

These discoveries have no direct connexion with those made in the Qumran caves. But they do have an important indirect bearing on the Qumran manuscripts. Many of the documents from Murabba'at and the unknown site in the same area are definitely dated in the second century A.D. The Biblical texts found along with them will not be later in date than these. It follows, in that case, that the Qumran manuscripts are earlier than the second century A.D., and that for two reasons. In the first place, the Murabba'at documents show a later stage in the evolution of Hebrew and Aramaic palaeography than the Qumran documents do. In the second place, the Biblical Hebrew texts at Murabbaʿat conform exactly to the consonantal text preserved by the later Massoretes; they reflect an age when textual deviations such as appear in several of the Biblical texts from Qumran had been removed from currency—largely, no doubt, through the activity of Rabbi Aqiba and his colleagues about the beginning of the second century. The Murabbaʿat texts, then, afford external confirmation of the general dating already established on other grounds for the Qumran manuscripts.

Khirbet Mird

Midway between the Wadi Qumran and the Wadi Murabbaʿat yet another watercourse runs down to the Dead Sea from the west—the Wadi en-Nar, better known to Bible readers as "the brook Kidron" which lies between Jerusalem and the Mount of Olives. From a ruined site to the north of this watercourse, Khirbet Mird, the indefatigable Taʿamireh unearthed further manuscript material of great interest, but of considerably later date than the documents found at Qumran and Murabbaʿat. These included papyrus fragments of private letters in Arabic from the seventh and eighth centuries, a Syriac letter (also on papyrus) written by a Christian monk, and a fragment of the *Andromache* of Euripides in Greek, together with a number of Biblical texts in Greek and Palestinian Syriac. The Greek texts included fragments of uncial codices of Wisdom, Mark, John and Acts, written between the fifth and eighth centuries A.D.; those in Palestinian Syriac included fragments of Joshua, Luke, John, Acts and Colossians (many of these were palimpsests). All these Biblical fragments were of Christian origin, unlike those from Qumran and Murabbaʿat, which belonged to Jews.

CHAPTER VI

THE SCROLLS AND THE OLD TESTAMENT

PLAINLY the Qumran sectaries were keen students of the Hebrew Scriptures. If we may judge from the fact that certain Old Testament books figured among the discoveries much more frequently than others, they would appear to have had a special interest in Deuteronomy, Isaiah, the Psalms, the Minor Prophets, and Daniel. But where so much has been left to the chances of time and tide, we can make but tentative inferences of this kind. Similarly, we cannot be too sure what to think of the fact that no fragment of the Book of Esther has been identified thus far among the Qumran finds. We know that some Jews, like some Christians in earlier and more recent times, had doubts about the fitness of Esther to be included in the canon of sacred books; on the other hand, the absence of any fragment of Esther from Qumran may be accidental, and indeed one might come to light unexpectedly.

The Canon of Scripture

Can we make any more general inferences about these people's views on the canon of holy writ? It is plain that they attached divine authority to the books of the first and second divisions of the Hebrew Bible—the Law and the Prophets. To them even such "minor prophets" as Micah, Nahum and Habakkuk were inspired oracles, foretelling things which they believed they could recognize as fulfilled in their own day. Very probably they attached similar authority to most of the books of the third division—the "Writings." But did they accept a wider canon than was officially acknowledged either in Jerusalem or at Alexandria? Their library included many apocalyptic and pseudepigraphic works which enjoyed considerable prestige among certain sections of the population of Judæa at that time, such as the *Book of Jubilees* and *First Enoch*. But it is not quite clear that they formally placed them on the same level as the Law and the Prophets. This is a matter which must receive further investigation. We have known Christians who in practice treated the Prayer Book or the *Pilgrim's Progress* as reverentially as they did the Bible; but this reverential treatment did not connote the formal canonization of these works. Such a work as the *Rule of the Community* was obviously intended to be binding on the community, but that would not make it holy scripture.

Literary Criticism

When the first news of the discoveries was released, their main significance was felt to lie in the new light which they might be expected to throw upon the text of the Old Testament. The reason for this has already been mentioned. If it was indeed true, as the first scholars to examine the scrolls claimed, that they belonged to the early years A.D., or the closing centuries B.C., then we had Hebrew Biblical manuscripts nearly a thousand years nearer to the time at which the Old Testament books were written than the earliest that were previously known. When further evidence seemed to confirm the early dating of the scrolls, a number of questions were eagerly asked. The first scroll to receive much publicity, and the first to be published in facsimile, was the complete manuscript of Isaiah from Cave 1. What fresh information could it supply about the problems arising from the study of that particular book? Did it prove, for example, that there were not "two Isaiahs," but one only?

To this question the scroll Isaiah A gives no answer which could tell us more than was known already. Even if it was copied out as early as 175 B.C., we knew that by that time the Book of Isaiah was current in practically its present form. For around the year 180 B.C. the Jewish sage Jesus Ben-Sira wrote his book of wisdom which we know as Ecclesiasticus; and in the section of that book entitled "The Praise of the Fathers," which celebrates the memory of great Israelites of earlier days, he makes it plain that the Book of Isaiah as known to him ran on at least to what we call Chapter 61. Speaking of King Hezekiah, who reigned in Judah during part of Isaiah's lifetime, Ben-Sira says (Ecclus. 48: 22–25):

For Hezekiah did that which was pleasing to the Lord,
  And was strong in the ways of David his father,
Which Isaiah the prophet commanded,

Who was great and faithful in his vision.
In his days the sun went backward;
And he added life to the king.
He saw by an excellent spirit what should come to pass at the last;
And he comforted them that mourned in Sion.
He shewed the things that should be to the end of time,
And the hidden things before ever they came.

In these lines Ben-Sira quotes indiscriminately from all parts of the Book of Isaiah. The reference to Isaiah's "vision" probably echoes Isaiah 1: 1; the reference to the sun's going backward and the adding of life to the king recalls the story of Hezekiah's sickness in Isa. 38; the prophet's seeing "what should come to pass at the last" may be an allusion to Isa. 2: 2; his comforting "them that mourned in Sion" is a combined reference to Isa. 40: 1 and 61: 3; and the last two lines of the quotation from Ben-Sira hark back to such passages as Isa. 41: 4, 22 f., 26 and 48: 6. So there is nothing surprising in the fact that a manuscript of Isaiah written rather later in the same century should contain the material of all sixty-six chapters, as Isaiah A does.

As soon as complete facsimiles of this scroll were available, many people looked up the place where Chapter 39 ends and Chapter 40 begins, and were impressed to find that there is no space between the two. In fact, Chapter 40 begins on the last line of a column. But this proves nothing. Those who think it does should be on their guard, lest they be invited to apply their own argument to an earlier part of the scroll. For Chapter 33 comes to an end near the foot of a column where there is still room for three lines of writing. But Chapter 34 does not begin immediately below the last line of Chapter 33; the space at the foot of the column is left blank, and Chapter 34 begins at the top of the following column. But has it ever been suggested that there is a change of authorship at the end of Chapter 33? Yes, indeed. In his lectures on *The Prophets of Israel*, for example (written in 1882), William Robertson Smith quoted the closing verses of Chapter 33 as containing the last message of "First Isaiah." "And so Jehovah's word to Isaiah ends, as it had begun," he says, "with the forgiveness of sins." But actually it would be as unsafe to argue that the space after Chapter 33 indicates a change of authorship there as it would be to argue that the absence of a space after Chapter 39 excludes a change of authorship there. The space after Chapter 33 might indicate rather a change of scribe, or it might have arisen if a scribe copied the first half of the book from one manuscript and the second half from another. In brief, the scroll tells us nothing at all about the stages by which our Book of Isaiah took its present form; and the only reason for dwelling on the matter at such length is that it has been suggested (even by people who ought to have known better) that this scroll gives a decisive answer to all our questions about the literary criticism of the book.

But certain theories of a few literary critics do seem to be put out of court by the scroll. One or two sections of Isaiah have been dated by some scholars in the Maccabean age—i.e. in the years following 168 B.C. One scholar thought that the portrayal of the Suffering Servant owed its inception to the suffering of the pious Jewish martyrs under Antiochus Epiphanes at that time; another dated Chapters 24 to 27 (the so-called "Isaiah Apocalypse") in the reign of John Hyrcanus (135–104 B.C.). It is certain that, if these extreme theories were well founded, these sections of Isaiah could never have been included in a manuscript of the book written about the middle of the second century B.C. But what are we to say of a scholar of our own time, who in the course of a study of the Dead Sea Scrolls found it possible to suggest that the portrayal of the Suffering Servant was based on the experience of the Teacher of Righteousness, the revered leader of the Qumran sect, whose death he assigned to 65 or 63 B.C.?[1]

Let us leave these questions of literary criticism, and turn to textual criticism, on which Isaiah A and the other Biblical manuscripts discovered at Qumran and Murabba'at have something more positive to say.

The Biblical Text

How do these earlier Biblical texts compare with those which we had hitherto known as the earliest surviving ones? Did the Jewish scribes who copied the sacred books generation after generation during the first nine centuries of the Christian era do their work accurately or carelessly? Did they introduce many mistakes? Do the newly discovered scrolls enable us to make large-scale corrections in the Massoretic manuscripts?

The new evidence confirms what we had already good reason

[1] See A. Dupont-Sommer, *The Dead Sea Scrolls* (1952), p. 96.

to believe—that the Jewish scribes of the early Christian centuries copied and recopied the text of the Hebrew Bible with the utmost fidelity. Their workmanship was much more accurate than the workmanship of the Christian scribes who copied and recopied the text of the Greek Bible.

The text of Isaiah A became available just in time for the translators of the Revised Standard Version of the Old Testament to make use of it before that version made its public appearance in September, 1952. Dr. Millar Burrows, who was a member of the Revision Committee, tells us[1] that thirteen readings in all were adopted in which Isaiah A deviates from the traditional text, and he adds that in some cases where he voted for the adoption of these readings he now thinks the traditional text ought to have been retained after all. One place where they were certainly right in adopting the reading of Isaiah A was in Isa. 21: 8, where the RSV says (in reference to a watchman who is looking out for the arrival of a messenger across the Syrian desert from the east): "Then he who saw cried: 'Upon a watchtower I stand, O Lord . . .'" There, by an accidental interchange of consonants, the Massoretic text has introduced the quite irrelevant figure of a lion, so that the AV reads, "And he cried, 'A lion . . .'," while the RV reads, "And he cried as a lion . . ."

But there is one place where we might certainly have expected the RSV to adopt a reading of Isaiah A—and there, remarkably enough, it has not even mentioned it in a footnote. In the oracle of the Suffering Servant in Chapter 53, verse 11 begins in the Massoretic text with the words which AV and RV render: "He shall see of the travail of his soul, and shall be satisfied." Now the Septuagint, the pre-Christian Greek translation of the Old Testament, adds the noun "light" as an object in the first clause of this verse, and it has generally been surmised that the Hebrew text originally had this word, but that it dropped out inadvertently in the course of copying and recopying. Critical editions of the Hebrew text regularly have a footnote at this point suggesting that the original reading was "From (or 'after') the travail of his soul he will see *light*, he will be satisfied." And this provides an answer to the reader's natural question when he considers the verse in the Massoretic text: "*What* will he see?" But now there is no need merely to *surmise* that the Hebrew

[1] *The Dead Sea Scrolls* (1955), pp. 304 ff.

text originally included the word "light"; it is there, plain for all to see, in the oldest known Hebrew manuscript—Isaiah A. And, as if that were not enough, it is present in the incomplete Isaiah manuscript which was also found in Cave 1—Isaiah B. There is no close relation between these two manuscripts, apart from the fact that they were stored in the same cave; and the fact that both have the word "light" in Isa. 53: 11 is exceedingly strong evidence that this is the original text. Yet the RSV strangely ignores this reading, and offers instead a paraphrase of the Massoretic text: "he shall see the fruit of the travail of his soul and be satisfied."

Another very attractive reading of Isaiah A which the RSV does not mention is in Isa. 40: 12, where we find "Who has measured *the waters of the sea* (Hebrew *mê yam*) in the hollow of his hand?" instead of the Massoretic "Who has measured *the waters* (Hebrew *mayim*) in the hollow of his hand?"

Isaiah A bears all the marks of a popular, unofficial copy of the sacred text. It was probably the work of amateur scribes, or at least of scribes who did not belong to the higher grades of their profession. The spelling is much more phonetic than the classical Hebrew spelling. Hebrew writing consisted originally of consonants only; the small dots and dashes which serve as vowel-points were not devised until the eighth and ninth centuries A.D. But at quite an early date some of the letters of the Hebrew alphabet (all of which had as their primary function the representation of consonantal sounds) were used for the secondary function of indicating certain important vowel-sounds. This use of vowel-letters appears as early as the inscription of Mesha, king of Moab, on the Moabite Stone (*c.* 850 B.C.), and readers of the Hebrew Bible are quite familiar with it. But it appears on a greatly extended scale in Isaiah A, and this was probably intended to help people who (unlike the regular readers in synagogues) were not expert in reading Hebrew. It has even been suggested, very reasonably, that the nationalist revival of Maccabean days probably promoted a renewal of interest in Hebrew as the traditional Jewish language, which had been displaced for many generations as a vernacular by the related Aramaic tongue. Jews who were trying to learn Hebrew afresh, like Zionists of more recent times, would naturally be glad of a more phonetic spelling than was practised in the schools.

For this reason Isaiah A throws incidental light on the pronunciation of Hebrew in Palestine in the second century B.C. Another minor respect in which it deviates from the traditional text is in certain grammatical forms and endings. An English analogy to this kind of deviation will be found if we compare forms like "saith" in the AV with "says" in the RSV. Here, too, the scroll provides some interesting information on the evolution of Hebrew inflexions. But deviations in spelling and accidence, of course, make no difference to the meaning, and disappear in the course of translation. Most of the deviations in Isaiah A which do make a difference to the meaning of the text—additions, omissions, and alterations of words and groups of words—simply show, when subjected to critical scrutiny, that the text of this manuscript, ancient as it is, is not so accurate as the traditional text which was received and handed on by the Massoretes.

As for Isaiah B, the differences between its text and that of the Massoretes are fewer and less significant. Whereas Isaiah A was probably copied by the eye (that is to say, from an earlier copy lying before the scribe or scribes), Isaiah B appears to have been copied by the ear (that is to say, someone read aloud from an older manuscript and the scribe wrote down what he heard, or what he thought he heard). Some of the scribal slips in Isaiah B are plainly due to faulty hearing. He found difficulty, for example, in distinguishing between the various guttural sounds in Hebrew. But he produced a much neater and more accurate piece of work than Isaiah A, which is rather slovenly by comparison. And, so far as the general impression made by the text of Isaiah B is concerned, it is as close to the traditional Massoretic text as makes no practical difference. That is one reason why its exhibition of the word "light" in Isa. 53: 11 is so noteworthy; clearly that word was present in the Hebrew text in general use at the beginning of the Christian era, and was dropped by accident at some point between then and A.D. 400 (it was absent from the Hebrew text on which Jerome based his Latin translation of the Old Testament at the beginning of the fifth century).

We have reason to believe, then, that the consonantal text of the Hebrew Bible which the Massoretes edited had been handed down to their time with conspicuous fidelity over a period of nearly a thousand years. There is some evidence that the text was revised about the beginning of the second century A.D. by

Rabbi Aqiba and his colleagues, who wished to see an authoritative text uniformly accepted by the Jewish people. But the testimony of these two manuscripts, which belong to a period earlier than Aqiba's generation, shows that the revising and editing which these scholars undertook cannot have involved any significant modification of the sacred writings. Perhaps they were concerned to exclude some eccentric texts which were in circulation, but in so far as they fixed a standard form, it was the form which was already widely accepted as standard.

We know that during the attack which was launched by Antiochus Epiphanes on the religious life of the Palestinian Jews in 168 B.C., the sacred scriptures were seized and destroyed by the king's officers. "They rent in pieces the books of the law which they found, and set them on fire; and wheresoever was found with any a book of the covenant, and if any consented to the divine law, the king's judgment delivered him to death" (I Macc. 1: 56 f.). It was inevitable, then, that when religious freedom was regained by the Jews a few years later, there should be an urgent call for new copies of the sacred books to replace those that were destroyed; not only would fresh copies be made but others would be imported from Jewish colonies outside Palestine. And while the exact course of events in this regard cannot be reconstructed, it appears quite probable that the form of text which the Massoretes inherited through the intervening generations from Aqiba and his contemporaries went back beyond their time to the Maccabean age.

As more and more copies of Hebrew Scripture were discovered at Qumran and Murabba'at and published for the benefit of the world of Biblical learning, it became evident that the Massoretic text was not the only form represented among them. The text of the Old Testament has come down to us along three main lines of transmission. One of these is the Massoretic line which has already been referred to. Another line is represented by the Greek translation called the Septuagint. We have excellent manuscripts of the Septuagint belonging to the fourth century A.D., very substantial fragments belonging to the century before that, and smaller fragments of even earlier date, the earliest being four fragmentary columns of a papyrus roll of Deuteronomy in Greek which was written in the second century B.C. It is well known that, when all allowances have been made for freedom and even inaccuracy in translation and for the use of paraphrase and interpretation in preference to a literal rendering of several passages, the Hebrew text from which the Septuagint version was made differed in many particulars from the traditional Hebrew text which has been handed down to us. It is natural to assume that the Septuagint version was based on copies of the Hebrew Bible which were current in Egypt (more especially, in Alexandria) in the last three centuries B.C., for it was primarily for the use of the Greek-speaking Jewish community of Alexandria that the Septuagint was produced. But it is only since the Qumran discoveries that copies of *Hebrew* Scripture have come to light which show readings formerly known only from the *Greek* Old Testament, and recognized as characteristic of the Septuagint.

Nor is that all. There was a third line of transmission along which one division of the Hebrew Bible was preserved. The Samaritans have preserved the Hebrew text of the Pentateuch in a recension of their own which goes back to the time when the breach between them and the Jews became final, shortly before the end of the period of Persian domination in the fourth century B.C. And some Hebrew Biblical texts found at Qumran have closer affinities with the recension hitherto regarded as distinctively Samaritan than with that which has been handed down in the Jewish tradition.

The conclusion to which we are forced is this: that all three forms of text—the Hebrew text received and transmitted by the Massoretes, the Hebrew text underlying the Septuagint, and the Hebrew text of the Pentateuch preserved by the Samaritans—were in no sense sectarian in the closing centuries of the Second Jewish Commonwealth, but were varying types of text current among the people of Israel in general, including the Jews of Palestine. It may be that the Massoretic text goes back to a Babylonian recension, while the Septuagint was based on the Hebrew text current in Egypt and the Samaritan was a Palestinian text. In any case, whatever differences might exist between the Qumran covenanters and their fellow-Jews, it is certain that they shared the same Biblical texts. If three distinguishable types of text were used at Qumran, that was because they were used elsewhere in Judæa. But from the later remains found at Murabba'at and its neighbourhood only one type of text is in evidence, so far as fragments of Hebrew Scripture are concerned. That is the

Massoretic type, and the reason may well be that Aqiba and his colleagues had established the Massoretic type as the one to be accepted, rather than the other two types represented at Qumran. And if Aqiba and his colleagues did in fact establish the Massoretic form of text as authoritative, we must applaud their sound judgment; for in the majority of places where one of the other forms deviates from the Massoretic reading, the Massoretic reading is superior.

When the Biblical fragments discovered by the archaeological explorers of Qumran Cave 1 in 1949 were studied, it was announced that a Hebrew fragment of Deuteronomy exhibited a reading in Ch. 31: 1 ("And Moses finished speaking all these words") which agreed with the Septuagint and not with the Massoretic text (which reads: "And Moses went and spoke these words"). But much more evidence of the same kind was forthcoming when the fragments from Cave 4 began to be examined. The best preserved Biblical document from Cave 4 is a Hebrew copy of the Books of Samuel. This scroll originally comprised fifty-seven columns, of which forty-seven have now been identified. This Hebrew text of Samuel is very much the type of text which the Septuagint translator of Samuel must have used. More remarkable still, it bears a close affinity to the text of Samuel which the author of the Books of Chronicles must have used in the composition of his work—closer than to the text of Samuel preserved in the Massoretic tradition.

A Hebrew fragment of Exodus agrees with the Septuagint against the Massoretic text by giving seventy-five instead of seventy as the number of Jacob's descendants in Ex. 1: 5 (compare Acts 7: 14).

A tiny fragment of Deut. 32: 8 exhibits for the first time documentary evidence for a Hebrew reading which has long been inferred on the basis of the Septuagint. In the Massoretic text this verse runs (as in the RV):

> When the Most High gave to the nations their inheritance,
> When he separated the children of men,
> He set the bounds of the peoples
> According to the number of the children of Israel.

The Septuagint reading of the last phrase is: "according to the number of the angels of God." From this it was concluded that the Hebrew text used by the Septuagint translator here did not have "children (sons) of Israel" but "sons of God" (in the sense in which that expression is used in Gen. 6: 2, 6; Job 1: 6; 2: 1; 38: 7). Many went further and regarded this a preferable reading to that of the Massoretic text. Thus the RSV renders the last phrase "according to the number of the sons of God," mentioning in a footnote that this is the reading implied by the Greek version, while the Hebrew has "Israel" and not "God." But now one fragmentary Hebrew manuscript can be cited in support of the reading "sons of God."

The end of the same chapter of Deuteronomy (the Song of Moses) exhibits in the Septuagint some marked divergencies from the Massoretic text. In particular, verse 43 is twice as long in the Septuagint version (and it is from a clause in the Septuagint of this verse which is absent from the Massoretic text that the words "Let all the angels of God worship him" are quoted in Heb. 1: 6). Another Hebrew fragment of Deut. 32 from Qumran Cave 4 runs from verse 37 to verse 43 and presents readings like those in the Septuagint which had not been found previously in any Hebrew manuscript.

From Cave 4 comes a fragmentary scroll of the Book of Exodus in Palaeo-Hebrew script which exhibits a type of text hitherto regarded as distinctively Samaritan. One of the distinctive features of the Samaritan Pentateuch is a persistent tendency to expansiveness. For example, if Moses is told to do something (for example, in connexion with the succeeding plagues of Egypt in the earlier chapters of Exodus), the Samaritan version is not content to say that "Moses did so"; it must go through all the details again as they are listed in the instructions given to Moses, and record how Moses carried them out one by one. Again, in the early chapters of Deuteronomy Moses rehearses in the first person a good part of the narrative of Exodus, but here and there in Moses' retrospect details are added which are absent from the traditional text of Exodus. The Samaritan text of Exodus inserts these. But these and other features formerly regarded as typically Samaritan are found in this scroll from Cave 4. We need not suppose that there was any special contact between the Qumran community and the Samaritans; what this and similar discoveries mean is that there was a time when this form of text was not peculiar to the Samaritans, but was current among the Jews as well.

And in addition to texts which can be classified quite distinctly as related to one or another of these three families (corresponding to the Massoretic, Septuagint and Samaritan editions) there are others which exhibit a mixture of features of two or more of these families, and it may be that some belong to other families which have not yet been identified. It will be a long time before a clear picture of the position is obtainable. But in general the new discoveries have increased our respect for the Massoretic Hebrew text. In a number of places it calls for emendation (the reading "he who saw" in Isa. 21: 8 and "light" in Isa. 53: 11 are certain emendations, and "sons of God" in Deut. 32: 8 a highly probable one); but over the whole area of the Old Testament writings its superiority to the other forms of text current at the end of the pre-Christian era is assured. The "great, indeed all-important question" which Sir Frederic Kenyon asked in 1939 is well on the way to receiving a much more explicit and positive answer than was thought possible then: "Does this Hebrew text, which we call Massoretic, and which we have shown to descend from a text drawn up about A.D. 100, faithfully represent the Hebrew text as originally written by the authors of the Old Testament books?"[1]

[1] *Our Bible and the Ancient Manuscripts*, p. 47.

CHAPTER VII

BIBLICAL INTERPRETATION AND THE MESSIANIC HOPE

Biblical Interpretation

ANOTHER question about the Qumran community's relation to the Old Testament leads us right into the heart of the community's life and faith. How did they *interpret* the Old Testament?

They interpreted it in such a way as to see their own duty in the perilous times through which they lived written clearly there for their instruction. This is immediately evident from one of the first scrolls to be unrolled—the Habakkuk commentary from Cave 1.[1] We have already seen how they reinterpreted the situation in which Habakkuk found himself, and saw in his words a description of their own circumstances.

There has never been any lack of people who have treated the Biblical prophecies in this way. In our own day we have seen how earnest Bible students thought they recognized in Hitler or Stalin the embodiment of the Antichrist foretold in the New Testament. In the early nineteen-thirties a gentleman in England, who edited a shortlived periodical to give currency to his highly individual interpretations of the Bible, published copies of letters which he had written to Mussolini and Einstein, informing them that they were respectively the Beast and the False Prophet—two sinister eschatological figures in the Book of Revelation. (Einstein sent him a brief and courteous reply, which was also published!) And throughout the Christian era there have been

[1] It must not be assumed that all the non-Biblical writings found at Qumran reflect the community's beliefs and practices. These writings (with the Biblical documents accompanying them) are the remains of the community's library, and no community would like it to be supposed that all the books in its library could be used as sources of information about its life and thought. But many of the non-Biblical works from Qumran do represent a self-consistent system of belief and practice, distinct from that of the main streams of Judaism, and in the light of other literary and archaeological evidence can reasonably be used to reconstruct the outlook and fortunes of the Qumran community.

serious people who believed, generation after generation, that their own days were the days of fulfilment, when history was to be wound up.

Our commentator, living some decades before the beginning of the Christian era, was sure that the time of the end was fast approaching, and that Habakkuk and the other prophets had prophesied primarily of the days which had now set in. Therefore he set himself to study and apply the words of Habakkuk according to what he believed to be their true meaning. That meaning was inevitably vague and mysterious until the time of fulfilment arrived; with its arrival, the meaning was plain for those who had eyes to see and hearts to understand. So he quotes the prophecy of Habakkuk, section by section, and adds the interpretation to each section as he goes along. Here is a sample of his method:[1]

(Hab. 1: 4) *So the law is slacked.*—The interpretation of this is that they have rejected the law of God.

And justice never goes forth, for the wicked surround the righteous.—The interpretation of this is that "the righteous" is the Teacher of Righteousness and "the wicked" is the Wicked Priest.

So justice goes forth perverted . . .

(1: 5) *Look among the nations, and see; wonder and be astounded: for I am doing a work in your days that you would not believe if told.*—The interpretation of this concerns wicked and deceitful men, with the Man of Falsehood, because they did not believe that which the Teacher of Righteousness had told them from the mouth of God; and it concerns those who acted deceitfully against the commandments of God and against the new covenant, because they did not believe in the covenant of God and did not keep His holy sabbath. And so the interpretation of the matter concerns those who act deceitfully in the latter days, violent men who break the covenant, who will not believe when they hear all that is coming upon the last generation from the mouth of the priest into whose heart God has put wisdom, to interpret all the words of His servants the prophets through whom He foretold what was to come upon His people and upon His land.

(1: 6) *For lo, I am rousing the Chaldaeans, that bitter and hasty nation.*—The interpretation of this concerns the Kitti'im, who are fleet and mighty in battle . . .

[1] Here and there in this "sample" a gap in the text has been filled in.

And so our commentator goes on; every sentence in the prophecy of Habakkuk is made to yield some reference to the two contrasted figures, the Wicked Priest and the Teacher of Righteousness, with their followers and associates, or else to the ruthless Kitti'im, who are sent by God to execute His judgment upon the oppressive rulers of His people, but who behave even more oppressively than those whom they put down.

Since the Kitti'im are plainly a world-power, pursuing a career of conquest and empire from the west, it may be thought that we shall have greater success in identifying them than in identifying Jewish individuals who, for all the importance which the commentator attached to them, may not have left their mark on the pages of history. Further details are given of their irresistible terror as the commentator explains how Habakkuk was really describing them when, to a superficial view, he was describing the Chaldaeans of his own day.

These Kitti'im, then, in their swift advance, overthrow all who stand in their way, and subdue them to their own dominion. They take possession of many lands and plunder the cities of the earth, "to seize habitations not their own," as Habakkuk says (1: 6). Nor do they rely on military power alone to accomplish their ends: "with deliberate counsel all their device is to do evil, and with cunning and deceit they proceed with all the nations" (this is a comment on 1: 7). "They trample the earth with their horses and their animals; they come from afar, from the coastlands of the sea, to devour all the nations vulture-wise, and they are never satisfied" (this on 1: 8). "With wrath and anger, with hot passion and fury, they speak to all the nations" (this on 1: 9). They mock at kings and potentates; they scoff at a mighty host; they laugh at fortresses, for they surround them with a large army and terrorize the defenders into surrender. This, too, is a sign of divine justice; these strongholds are surrendered because of the iniquity of those who dwell in them (all this is by way of a comment on 1: 10). Yet these Kitti'im have rulers who follow one another in quick succession; "they come one after another to destroy the earth" (this on 1: 11).

When Habakkuk describes the Chaldaeans as netting men like fish (1: 15), the commentator explains that the Kitti'im "gather their wealth with all their plunder like the fish of the sea." And when the prophet goes on to say that the Chaldaeans thereupon pay divine honours to the nets in which they have taken their captives (1: 16), the commentator says that the Kitti'im sacrifice to their standards and regard their weapons of war with religious veneration. They impose heavy tribute on the nations, to be paid year by year, thus denuding the lands of their wealth. And in war they are completely pitiless: their sword spares neither men, women, nor the tiniest children.

It is difficult to avoid the conclusion that these Kitti'im are the Romans. Several of the individual points in the description would be applicable to other conquerors, but the whole impression can scarcely be said to fit any other conquering people of whom we know. Alexander's invasion of Asia is too early for other elements in the picture, and cannot be related to several details in the description of the Kitti'im. His successors, the Ptolemies and Seleucids, who battled in Palestine did not come from "the coastlands of the sea" (i.e. from the Aegean and Mediterranean shores) but from Egypt and Syria. The rulers of the Kitti'im, who followed one another in quick succession, "by the counsel of a guilty house,"[1] may remind us of the chief magistrates of Rome, elected annually to serve for a year; in the Near East, during the first century B.C., one Roman commander-in-chief was displaced by another with disconcerting suddenness and frequency. While the statement that the Kitti'im pay divine honours to their standards and weapons may be a rhetorical exaggeration, it is a fact that the "eagles" and other standards of the Roman army were regarded as sacred objects. The "eagle," the standard of a legion, was kept in a special shrine in the military camp and was regarded as affording sanctuary. When the legionaries under Titus stormed the Jerusalem temple in A.D. 70, Josephus describes how they set up their standards over against the eastern gate and offered sacrifices to them there.

At one time it was thought that in another of the scrolls from Cave 1, the *Rule of War*, where the term Kitti'im also occurs, the reference must certainly be to the Seleucids and the Ptolemies, because a distinction was made between the Kitti'im of Assyria and the Kitti'im in Egypt. But when the complete scroll was published, this interpretation no longer seemed so inevitable, for the "Kitti'im of Assyria" could reasonably be understood of the Roman administration of Syria and the "Kitti'im in Egypt" of

[1] A reference to the Roman senate?

the Roman forces in Egypt, the more so as the *Rule of War* appears to have been written in the earlier part of the Roman occupation of Judæa.

But the reference to the *Rule of War* gives us a further opportunity of illustrating the belief of the Qumran community that they were living in the last days, and that all the things foretold by the prophets were due to be fulfilled in the very near future.

As they read the prophets, they gathered that the last days were to be marked by a final and decisive conflict, of unprecedented bitterness, between the forces of right and the forces of wrong. In Chapters 38 and 39 of Ezekiel, for example, they read of an invasion of Palestine from the north, led by one Gog, ruler of the land of Magog. Gog would march at the head of a vast international host, which would be annihilated by divine intervention. Probably when Alexander the Great marched south along the Syro-Palestinian coastal road from Asia Minor some Jewish thinkers identified him with Gog, but the event proved them wrong. But this time, surely, the identification could not be in doubt!

Again, as they read the Book of Daniel, they read in the closing verses (36–45) of Chapter 11 about a self-willed king from the north who would establish dominion over Egypt, Libya and the Sudan, and then turn back from there to pitch his camp with hostile intent west of Jerusalem; "yet he shall come to his end, with none to help him." Those days would be days of unparalleled affliction for the faithful in Israel, and they would owe their deliverance to the intervention of Michael the archangel as their champion.

The men of Qumran believed firmly that these days of unparalleled affliction were imminent. The last warfare of all was about to break out—the struggle, as they called it, "of the sons of light against the sons of darkness." But, even if they could expect Michael to arise as their champion and bring them final victory, they must not remain passive in this critical hour; they must go forth to the help of the Lord against the mighty. To do this effectively they must study the art of war. And the results of their study are set down in the *Rule of War*. In the twentieth chapter of Deuteronomy they found regulations for the ancient institution of the holy war in Israel; these, they decided, must be brought up to date and put into practice, for the expected battle was not theirs, but the Lord's. The military technique of those far-distant days when their ancestors invaded Canaan under the leadership of Joshua, however, would not be adequate for the situation in which the men of Qumran now found themselves. Accordingly, they set themselves to study the contemporary art of war, with the aid of the most up-to-date Roman military manuals. With this remarkable combination of ancient religion and modern technique they prepared to sustain a forty years' war. (But, in accordance with the ancient law of holy war, they would abstain from hostilities every seventh year.) At an early stage in the war they would return from "the wilderness of the peoples" where they lived in exile to encamp in "the wilderness of Jerusalem" and give battle to the Kitti'im and their allies. After the overthrow of these enemies, they would deal with the Kitti'im in Egypt, and the dominion of the Kitti'im would disappear completely. A pure sacrificial worship would be restored in Jerusalem, under acceptable priests. The warfare would be continued against other "sons of darkness"—the ancestral enemies of Israel in seven of the surrounding lands. There would be seven major campaigns; in three of these the sons of light would conquer and in three they would be vanquished, but the seventh time final victory would be secured for them through the intervention of Michael. The men of Belial would be annihilated; the triumph of the people of God, foretold by so many of the prophets of old, would be achieved; everlasting righteousness would be brought in; the kingdom of heaven would be established in perpetuity. In words which echoed the ancient victory-songs of Old Testament and Maccabean times they sang in advance the chant of welcome with which the conquering hero, the captain of the Lord's host, would be received after his victory over the sons of darkness:

> Arise, O mighty man, and lead thy captivity captive, thou man of glory!
> Gather thy plunder, O thou who doest valiantly!
> Set thy hand on the necks of thy foes
> And thy foot on the heaps of the slain!
> Smite through the nations, thy adversaries,
> And let thy sword devour the flesh of guilty man.
> Fill thy land with glory,
> And thy heritage with blessing;

Let there be a multitude of cattle in thy camps,
Silver and gold and precious stones in thy palaces!
O Zion, rejoice exceedingly;
Shine forth with ringing shouts, O Jerusalem;
And be joyful, all ye cities of Judah!
Open thy gates continually,
That they may bring into thee the wealth of nations,
And their kings may serve thee;
All who have oppressed thee shall pay thee homage
And lick the dust of thy feet.
O daughters of my people, sing with a voice of ringing joy;
Deck yourselves with ornaments of glory and beauty!

The Messianic Hope

We know that in certain forms of Jewish expectation the final victory over the enemies of Israel and the establishment of the kingdom of God was closely associated with a Messiah. The term "Messiah," let us remind ourselves, means "Anointed One"; and anyone who is so designated holds his office "by divine right" or "by the grace of God." Thus even a pagan monarch like Cyrus could be addressed as the "Messiah" of the God of Israel (Isa. 45: 1) because he had been raised up in order to fulfil God's purpose, and by his policy and activity he was energetically promoting that purpose, however little he was aware of the fact. But the title is given pre-eminently to the kings of David's dynasty, and in later times was used of an expected ruler of that dynasty who would restore and surpass the vanished glories of David's imperial days.

In one interesting work, which some scholars nowadays are inclined to associate fairly closely with the Qumran outlook—*The Testaments of the Twelve Patriarchs*[1]—a notable part in the victory and restoration of the last days is given to a Messiah of the tribe of Levi, who stands alongside the Davidic Messiah (the Messiah of the tribe of Judah) and in fact overshadows him.

What light do the Qumran texts throw on the community's

[1] This is a pre-Christian Jewish work which has come down to us in a form containing several Christian interpolations. It has been widely held that in its original form it spoke of a Levitical Messiah only, and that the references to a Messiah of the tribe of Judah have been interpolated at a later date. More probably both Messiahs figured in the work from the beginning. Fragments of an earlier Aramaic form of the *Testament of Levi* have been found in Caves 1 and 4 at Qumran.

messianic expectation? What part is played, for example, in that expectation by the "mighty man" who is addressed in the victory chant which has just been quoted? Is he to be identified with the Messiah?

In the *Rule of the Community* it is laid down that the community in question shall continue to live under its original rule "until the coming of a prophet and the anointed ones (Messiahs) of Aaron and Israel" (column 9, line 11). These are presumably figures whose advent is expected to mark the epoch for which the community was making preparation. Further light is thrown upon this expectation by the contents of a document found in Cave 4.

This brief document brings together a few passages from the Old Testament which formed the basis for certain messianic expectations. It begins with the passage in Deut. 18: 18–19 where God says to Moses: "I will raise up for them [i.e. for the people of Israel] a prophet like you from among their brethren." (To this passage it appends Deut. 5: 28–29.) Next comes a quotation from Num. 24: 15–17, where the Mesopotamian prophet Balaam foresees the rise of a military conqueror in Israel (probably King David):

> I see him, but not now;
> I behold him, but not nigh:
> a star shall come forth out of Jacob,
> and a sceptre shall rise out of Israel;
> it shall crush the forehead of Moab,
> and break down all the sons of Sheth.

This is followed by the blessing pronounced by Moses upon the tribe of Levi (the priestly tribe) in Deut. 33: 8–11, which begins with the words:

> Give to Levi thy Thummim,
> and thy Urim to thy godly one.

(The Thummim and the Urim constituted the oracular equipment by means of which the chief priest in early Israel ascertained the divine will.)[1]

[1] After these three quotations comes a concluding one from a hitherto unknown work provisionally named the *Psalms of Joshua*.

The way in which these three quotations are brought together suggests that the writer looked forward to the advent of a great prophet, a great captain, and a great priest. And this threefold expectation is certainly related to the words already quoted from the *Rule of the Community*. The expected prophet is obviously common to both; as for the "anointed ones of Aaron and Israel," these are doubtless to be identified with the two other figures envisaged in the collection of Biblical quotations—the great priest being the "Messiah of Aaron" and the great captain the "Messiah of Israel" (identical in all probability with the Davidic Messiah).

In this connexion it is interesting to note that one of the names by which the community described itself was the community of Israel and Aaron (i.e. laymen and priests). And it probably expected both the Messiah of Israel and the Messiah of Aaron to emerge from its own ranks.

In the two "Zadokite" documents—the *Admonition* and the *Laws*—several references are made to the "Messiah of Aaron and Israel" who was expected to arise in the end of the days. It is now considered by a number of scholars that the singular term probably replaced an original plural in the course of transmission, to bring the language into line with current Jewish doctrine.

The "mighty man" of the *Rule of War* might well be the expected "Messiah of Israel" in whom the community apparently recognized Balaam's "star out of Jacob"; but alongside him in the *Rule of War* there stands the high priest, who is apparently his superior. Similarly, in a collection of benedictions discovered in Cave 1, there is a blessing for the high priest and one for the "prince of the congregation." And in another document from the same cave, entitled the *Rule of the Congregation*,[1] the order of precedence is laid down for a banquet which appears to have its setting in the new age. The Messiah of Israel is there, but he occupies a subordinate place to the priest. "Let no one begin to eat bread or drink wine before the priest, for it is his province to bless the first mouthful of bread and wine and to stretch forth his hands first upon the bread. Thereafter the Messiah of Israel may stretch forth his hands upon the bread." This reminds us forcibly of the subordinate position of the "prince" to the priesthood in the programme for the new

[1] A companion document to the *Rule of the Community*, but distinct from it.

commonwealth set out in the last nine chapters of the Book of Ezekiel.

In ancient Israel two outstanding offices were "messianic" in the sense that men were appointed to these offices by the solemn ceremony of anointing. These were the priesthood and the kingship. The king of Israel was known as "the LORD's anointed," but the priest (more especially the chief priest) was also known as "the anointed." To both is accorded the Hebrew designation *mashiach* (Messiah), which is translated in the Septuagint, the Greek version of the Old Testament, as *christos* (Christ). Both priest and king were in their varying ways mediators between God and their people, and so was the prophet, although he was not regularly installed in his prophetic office by anointing. (Elijah's command, in I Kings 19: 16, to anoint Elisha to be prophet in his place is exceptional.) Even the prophets, however, could be described collectively as God's anointed men, because they acted under His commission, even if no oil had been poured on their heads. Thus, in Psa. 105: 15—

> Touch not my anointed ones,
> do my prophets no harm!—

the parallelism shows that "anointed ones" (Messiahs) and "prophets" are synonymous terms. And there are a couple of places in the Zadokite *Admonition* and one in the *Rule of War* where the expression "anointed ones" appears with the evident meaning of "prophets."

In any case, we have found an interesting point of contact between Qumran and Christianity—a point of contact which is also a point of cleavage. The Qumran community and the early Christians agreed that in the days of the fulfilment of all that the Old Testament prophets had said there would arise a great prophet, a great captain and ruler, and a great priest. But these three figures remained distinct in Qumran expectation, whereas the early Christians saw them unified in the person of Christ. The threefold office of Christ as Prophet and Priest and King, a well-established theme in traditional Christian theology, is implicit in various early strands of New Testament teaching.

It is worth while, however, to look at the three passages quoted on the leaf from Cave 4 in the light of the early Christian interpretation of the Old Testament.

The first quotation, the passage about the prophet whom God would raise up as He had raised up Moses, is referred to several times in the New Testament. According to John 1: 21, a deputation which came from Jerusalem to interview John the Baptist during his baptismal ministry in the Jordan valley asked him if he claimed to be one or another of the various figures who were expected to arise in Israel at the time of fulfilment. Was he the Messiah? Was he Elijah (who was expected to return to earth shortly before the Messiah appeared)?[1] But when he assured them that he was neither the Messiah nor Elijah, they asked him, "Are you the prophet?" And he answered, "No." He did not need to ask, "Which prophet?" He knew at once which prophet they meant—the prophet of whom Moses spoke in Deut. 18: 15 ff.

The same Evangelist tells us that when Jesus had fed the multitude with loaves and fishes by the Sea of Galilee, the people said: "This is indeed the prophet who is to come into the world!" (John 6: 14). They linked the food with which Jesus had just fed them with the manna which their forefathers ate in the wilderness in the days of Moses: surely this must be the new prophet, the second Moses! Again, when three of Jesus' disciples saw the vision of Jesus in glory along with Moses and Elijah, on the mount of transfiguration, they heard a heavenly voice directing their attention to Jesus: "This is my beloved Son; listen to him" (Mark 9: 7). Those words, "listen to him," echo the words of Moses in Deut. 18: 15 ("The LORD your God will raise up for you a prophet like me from among you, from your brethren—*him you shall heed*") and mark Jesus out as the prophet whom Moses had in mind.

This identification of Jesus with the prophet like Moses finds even more explicit expression in the early chapters of the Book of the Acts: once in Acts 3: 22, where Peter, in the court of the Jerusalem temple, quotes the actual words of Moses from Deut. 18 and refers them to Jesus, and once in Acts 7: 37, where Stephen, on trial for his life before the Sanhedrin, quotes the same words as a prediction of Jesus.

Balaam's prophecy about the star out of Jacob was plainly a favourite with the Qumran community. It appears not only on the leaf from Cave 4, but also in two major community docu-

[1] See p. 127.

ments. In the Zadokite *Admonition* (column 7, lines 19 f.) the "star" and the "sceptre" (which in the original oracle are variant symbols for one and the same figure) are dissociated: the "star" is "the Expounder of the Law" (sometimes identified with the Teacher of Righteousness), but the "sceptre" is "the prince of all the congregation," that is to say, the military leader. The oracle is also interpreted of the military leader in the *Rule of War* (column 11, line 6), in the course of a hymn of thanksgiving to God: "Thine is the warfare; from thee is the strength; it is not ours; it is not our might or the power of our hands that has wrought valiantly, but by thy might and the strength of thy great valour, even as thou hast made it known to us from of old, saying: 'A star shall come forth out of Jacob, and a sceptre shall rise out of Israel . . .'" Here the conquest foretold in the oracle is identified with the expected victory over the Kitti'im and other sons of darkness.

This passage from Num. 24: 17 does not figure among the messianic prophecies applied to Jesus in the New Testament (unless there is a distant allusion to it in the title "the bright morning star" in Rev. 22: 16). But it was soon seized upon by Christians as one of the scriptures which bore witness to Him. Thus the Christian apologist and philosopher Justin Martyr, in his *Dialogue with Trypho the Jew* (Chapter 106), says: "And that He [Jesus] should arise like a star from the seed of Abraham, Moses showed beforehand when he said: 'A star shall arise out of Jacob, and a leader from Israel.'" Justin's citation of these words was the more significant at the time (*c.* A.D. 135), for Trypho had lately escaped from the disastrous fighting in Palestine which followed Rabbi Aqiba's recognition of the messianic claimant Simeon Ben-Kosebah as the "star out of Jacob" (whence his new patronymic Bar-Kokhba).[1] So Num. 24: 17 was interpreted of the Messiah by a leader in the main stream of Jewish tradition as well as by the Qumran covenanters and the Christians.

If, however, the New Testament writers did not invoke the Balaam oracle as a prophecy fulfilled by Jesus, they did apply to Him other Old Testament passages which similarly depict a mighty conqueror. Outstanding among these are Psa. 2 and 110. In the former of these the Davidic king, the LORD's anointed, says:

[1] See pp. 13, 53 ff.

I will tell of the decree of the LORD:
He said to me, "You are my son,
today I have begotten you.
Ask of me, and I will make the nations your heritage,
and the ends of the earth your possession.
You shall break them with a rod of iron,
and dash them in pieces like a potter's vessel."

In the latter the psalmist addresses the king thus:

The Lord is at your right hand;
he will shatter kings on the day of his wrath.
He will execute judgment among the nations,
filling them with corpses;
he will scatter chiefs
over the wide earth.[1]

Such passages could be applied quite literally in the Qumran documents to the valiant hero who would lead the faithful to victory in the war against the sons of darkness; that the early Christians could apply them to Jesus shows how thoroughly (under His influence, of course) they had transmuted their military significance. After all, the most convinced Christian pacifists of our day sing quite cheerfully hymns like *Onward! Christian soldiers* and *Fight the good fight* because the warfare to which these words refer is waged against spiritual enemies. We may wonder idly what some archaeologist of two thousand years hence will make of a fragment of Sankey's hymn-book when he finds the first hymn in the collection opening with these words:

Ho, my comrades! see the signal
Waving in the sky!
Reinforcements now appearing;
Victory is nigh!

We can imagine what ludicrous mistakes he may well make; but are we making similarly ludicrous mistakes in our interpretation of the Qumran *Rule of War*? Probably not; for the *Rule of War*

[1] These particular words from Psa. 110 are not quoted in the New Testament, but the priest-king to whom they are addressed is repeatedly identified with the Christian Messiah (cf. Mark 12: 36; Acts 2: 34 f.; I Corinthians 15: 25; Heb. 1: 13; 5: 6, etc.).

is mainly prose, not poetry; and the military language seems too direct and circumstantial to be allegorical.

As for the passage from Deut. 33 which our document from Cave 4 quotes as forecasting a priestly Messiah, neither this nor any other Old Testament mention of the Levitical priesthood is applied to our Lord in the New Testament. The reason is not far to seek; one New Testament writer expresses it succinctly when he says: "it is evident that our Lord was descended from Judah, and in connexion with that tribe Moses said nothing about priests" (Heb. 7: 14). He could not be hailed as a "Messiah of Aaron." No one in apostolic times, so far as we can gather, ascribed to Him a priestly heritage on the ground that His mother was related to the mother of John the Baptist, who was "of the daughters of Aaron" (Luke 1: 5)—although this argument was brought forward at a later date. There is some evidence, indeed, that certain Jewish Christians denied the legitimacy of the Jerusalem priesthood and regarded James the Just and other members of the holy family as the true high priests of the new Israel; but this was not based on any claim to Aaronic descent but on their relationship to Jesus. But when the New Testament ascribes a priestly status to Jesus, it does so on totally different grounds. The writer of the Epistle to the Hebrews finds Old Testament authority for the priestly side of Jesus' messianic work in Psa. 110: 4, where a prince of the house of David is hailed by God as "a priest for ever after the order of Melchizedek." There was sound historical justification for ascribing a priesthood of this order to the Davidic Messiah, for it is extremely probable that after David's capture of Jerusalem he and his successors viewed themselves as heirs to the ancient royal priesthood exercised by Melchizedek and other pre-Israelite rulers of that city. The writer to the Hebrews does not dwell on this historical basis for his argument (perhaps he was not greatly interested in it); but by developing the doctrine of Jesus' perpetual priesthood in terms of the Old Testament portrayal of Melchizedek he has given the Christian Church its classic exposition of this phase of our Lord's messianic dignity and service.

The Qumran community, then, had its messianic doctrine. One point in which it differs from the messianic doctrine of the New Testament, as we have said, is its expectation of three distinct personages at the end of the age, whereas the Christian

Messiah was Prophet and Priest and King in one. But there is a more important point of difference than that. There is a constant danger of confusion when we use the term "Messiah," because in the Christian tradition our ideas of what is meant by it are determined by the life and work of Jesus. But in fact His life and work have quite changed the meaning of the term. It was no doubt because of the meaning which was popularly attached to it by those among whom He moved that Jesus Himself, except on rare and significant occasions, did not make use of it. His hearers would have been misled if He had done so. He knew Himself to be Messiah-designate from the moment of His baptism, if not before. But from the same moment, if not before, He also knew that His Messiahship must be fulfilled in terms of the obedient and suffering Servant of the Lord. The messianic figures whom we meet in the Qumran documents do not achieve their destiny in this manner. There was indeed a most moving interpretation of the Servant Songs accepted by the Qumran community, but it does not appear to have influenced the way in which they envisaged the great messianic figures of the end-time. But all the phases of our Lord's messianic ministry receive their distinctive quality from the historical figure of the Son of Man, who came not to be served by others but to be a Servant Himself, and to give His life a ransom for many.

CHAPTER VIII

THE TEACHER OF RIGHTEOUSNESS AND HIS ENEMIES

A COMPREHENSIVE scheme of Biblical interpretation such as the Qumran community followed is not likely to have arisen by accident. It bears the impress of an original mind, and we are told quite plainly whose mind this was.

The Zadokite *Admonition* tells how a righteous remnant of the people of Israel, probably in the second century before Christ, realized that they were involved in the general national apostasy, and decided to renew the ancient covenant with the God of their fathers. But for some time they were uncertain what course of life they should adopt in order to maintain their loyalty to the covenant. After twenty years, however, God raised up a "Teacher of Righteousness" who taught them the true way of life. Not only so, but this Teacher of Righteousness was given special insight into the purpose of God, so that he was able to make known to the "last generations" what God was going to accomplish in the "last generation." And it was evidently to the Teacher of Righteousness that our community owed its distinctive interpretation of Old Testament prophecy, as well as its organization by camps like a miniature Israel in the wilderness, its rigorous discipline and its expectation of the near advent of the day of the Lord.

With this agrees much of what is said about the Teacher of Righteousness in the Habakkuk commentary found in Cave 1. As we have seen, the warnings of judgment in Habakkuk's oracle are directed by the commentator against those who refuse to believe "that which the Teacher of Righteousness had told them from the mouth of God." And when the commentator goes on to denounce those covenant-breakers "who will not believe when they hear all that is coming upon the last generation from the mouth of the priest into whose heart God has put wisdom, to interpret all the words of His servants the prophets through whom He foretold what was to come upon His people and upon His land," we naturally understand by the "priest" either the Teacher of Righteousness in person or else someone who perpetuated his interpretation of Scripture after his decease (in which case the "priest" might be the commentator himself).

In Hab. 2: 1–2 the prophet describes how, in his perplexity to comprehend the purpose of God, he determined to wait for the further light that might come with the unfolding of God's purpose in history, and received a fresh assurance from God that the final vindication of righteousness would not be long delayed. "I will take my stand to watch, and station myself on the tower, and look forth to see what he will say to me, and what I will answer concerning my complaint. And the LORD answered me: 'Write the vision; make it plain upon tablets, so he may run who reads it. . . .'" Here is the commentator's interpretation of this passage:

> God told Habakkuk to write the things that were to come upon the last generation, but the fulfilment of the appointed time He did not make known to him. And as for the words, "so that he may run who reads it," their interpretation concerns the Teacher of Righteousness, to whom God made known all the mysteries of the words of His servants the prophets.

That is to say, Habakkuk was enabled to foresee what was going to happen in the end-time, but he was not told when the end-time would arrive. But when the Teacher of Righteousness arose, God revealed to him that the end-time was at hand, and showed him how the predictions of Habakkuk and the other prophets were about to be fulfilled. For, it was believed, all the prophets had spoken of the end-time rather than of their own days. If Isaiah, for example, announced the downfall of the enemy of the people of God in the words, "And the Assyrian shall fall by a sword, not of man; and a sword, not of man, shall devour him" (Isa. 31: 6), he was not so much referring to the overthrow of Sennacherib's army in his own day (701 B.C.) as to the defeat of the Kitti'im by the sons of light at the end of the age. In fact, the words which Peter the apostle used of the foundation-events of Christianity could equally well have been used by the exegetes of Qumran to express their own belief: "Moses . . . and all the prophets who have spoken, from Samuel and those who came afterwards, also proclaimed these days" (Acts 3: 22, 24).

Who, then, was this Teacher of Righteousness, whose original and creative interpretation of Hebrew Scripture so influenced the thought and life of the community which revered him as its leader?

At present he cannot be identified certainly with any historical figure known to us from other sources. We can, however, piece together the fragments of information about him supplied by the texts which mention him, so as to obtain a fairly clear impression of the kind of man he was.

We have already seen that, in the belief of his followers, he had been initiated into the mysteries of the divine purpose and enabled to understand the true interpretation of the prophets of old.[1] What he had thus learned from God he imparted to his disciples. In a fragmentary commentary on the Book of Micah, found in Cave 1, the Teacher of Righteousness is described as "the one who teaches the law to his people and to all who offer themselves to be gathered into the elect people of God, practising the law in the council of the community, who will be saved from the day of judgment." Plainly, then, his disciples did not listen to him for instruction alone, but took practical steps to act upon his teaching, and believed that by doing so they would enjoy deliverance when the approaching judgment day arrived. In fact, the well-known words "The righteous shall live by his faith" (Hab. 2:4) are interpreted in the Qumran commentary on Habakkuk as referring to "all the doers of the law in the house of Judah, whom God will deliver from the house of judgment (i.e. will justify) because of their travail and their faith in the Teacher of Righteousness." Similarly, at the end of the Zadokite *Admonition*, the promise is made that "all who hold fast to these rules, to go out and to come in according to the law, and who listen to the voice of the Teacher and make confession before God, saying, 'Verily, we have done wickedly, both we and our fathers, in walking contrary to the ordinances of the covenant; just and true are thy judgments against us'; who do not act high-handedly against His holy ordinances and righteous judgments and truthful testimonies; who learn from the former judgments wherewith the men of the community were judged; who hearken to the voice of the Teacher of Righteousness and do not repudiate the ordinances of righteousness when they hear them;—they shall rejoice

[1] Some of the Qumran *Hymns of Thanksgiving* appear to describe the Teacher's religious experiences in the first person.

and be glad and their heart shall be strong, and they shall win the mastery over all the children of the world, and God shall make propitiation for them, and they shall see His salvation, for they have put their trust in His holy name."

On the other hand, those who disregarded the words of the Teacher of Righteousness were believed to have forfeited all hope of salvation.

The appearance of the Teacher of Righteousness was taken to be a sign that the closing period of the present age had set in. He was not the Messiah, but his activity meant that the messianic epoch could not be long delayed. An unspecified interval separated the "gathering in" (i.e. the death) of the Teacher from "the rise of a Messiah from Aaron and from Israel," according to the Zadokite *Admonition*. It may well be that the word "Messiah" originally appeared in the plural number in this text; but in any case the Teacher played the part of a forerunner, "to make ready for the Lord a people prepared," rather than the part of a Messiah. The unspecified interval separating his "gathering in" from the rise of the messianic personage or personages referred to may have been forty years; at least we are told a few lines lower down in the *Admonition* that "from the day when the unique Teacher was gathered in until the destruction of all the men of war who returned with the man of falsehood is about forty years." The identification of "the men of war who returned with the man of falsehood" is a highly speculative matter, but their destruction was probably expected to be one of the events to take place on the very eve of the messianic appearing. It is possible that the Teacher's disciples expected that he would rise from the dead at the end of this interval, and resume his teaching ministry by clearing up all problems of legal interpretation hitherto left unsolved. (In the main stream of Jewish belief this rôle was reserved for Elijah, who was expected to return at the end of the age as Messiah's precursor.) But there is no suggestion that the Teacher would be accorded messianic status, even after his resurrection from the dead.

Can we say anything about the time at which the Teacher flourished? If we could identify some of his contemporaries who are alluded to in the Habakkuk commentary, we might be able to give him an approximate date; but we have to reckon with the tantalizing vagueness with which these contemporaries are mentioned.

Of these contemporaries one is repeatedly described as the Wicked Priest, an implacable adversary of the Teacher of Righteousness. There was one outstanding occasion on which the Wicked Priest showed his hostility: this was when he "pursued after the Teacher of Righteousness to his place of exile, to swallow him up in his hot fury, and on the occasion of the appointed season of rest, the day of atonement, he burst upon them to swallow them up and to make them stumble on the fast-day, their sabbath of rest." This allusion can be more easily understood when we bear in mind that the Teacher and his followers appear to have observed a different religious calendar from that by which the sacred year was regulated in the temple at Jerusalem. We gather, then, that on the occasion referred to the Teacher and his community were observing the Great Day of Atonement in their wilderness retreat according to their reckoning of the day, when the Wicked Priest, for whom it was an ordinary day, invaded their meeting-place in order to throw them into confusion and make them sin by doing acts which ought not to be done on a "sabbath of rest."[1]

But the Wicked Priest was overtaken at last by a fearful fate, in which the community discerned the hand of divine justice. "Because of the evil done to the Teacher of Righteousness and the men of his council, God gave him into the hands of his enemies, to afflict him with a stroke, to make him waste away in bitterness of soul, because he acted wickedly against His elect." In this the commentator sees the fulfilment of the prophet's words: "Will not your debtors suddenly arise, and those awake who will make you tremble?" (Hab. 2: 7). But he gives these words a somewhat different sense: "Will not those who bite you suddenly arise, and will not your tormentors awake?" Then he says:

[1] The Jewish year, according to the traditional calendar (which survives for religious purposes to the present day), consists of twelve months which alternately have thirty and twenty-nine days (corresponding to the moon's circuit of the earth, which is completed in about twenty-nine and a half days). This yields 354 days to a year; the approximate difference of eleven and a quarter days required to make up the solar year is provided for by the insertion of a thirteenth month every few years. But the Qumran community probably used the calendar followed in the *Book of Jubilees*, in which the year consisted of 364 days (exactly fifty-two weeks), with twelve months of thirty days each and an extra day added each quarter. The Sadducees and Pharisees disagreed about certain festival datings, but they accepted the same general calendar; the Qumran covenanters differed radically from them both. In the Qumran calendar a festival would fall in each year on the same day of the week.

"The interpretation of this concerns the priest who rebelled and transgressed the ordinances of God . . . therefore they smote him with judgments of wickedness, and wrought horrors of sore diseases upon him, and vengeance upon his body of flesh."

It may be questioned, indeed, if we ought without more ado to identify "the priest who rebelled and transgressed the ordinances of God" with the man elsewhere called the Wicked Priest, but on the whole the identification seems probable enough.

The Wicked Priest had not always been so blatantly wicked as (in the eyes of our commentator and his associates) he later turned out to be. "He was called according to the name of truth when first he arose, but when he ruled in Israel his heart was lifted up and he forsook God and betrayed the ordinances for the sake of wealth. He looted and piled up the wealth of the violent men who rebelled against God; and he took the wealth of nations, bringing upon himself more iniquity and guilt, and he acted in abominable ways, with every defiling impurity." This is amplified in the comment on Hab. 2: 16, 17. Verse 16 is said to refer to "the priest whose shame was greater than his glory, because he did not circumcise his heart but walked in the ways of drunkenness to quench his thirst. But the cup of God's wrath will overwhelm him, bringing more shame and ignominy upon him." The following verse (17) was apparently read thus by the commentator: "The violence done to Lebanon will overwhelm you; the destruction of the beasts will terrify you, for the blood of men and violence to the land, to a city and all who dwell therein." For this is how he explains it: "The interpretation of this saying refers to the Wicked Priest, to repay him his recompense as he recompensed the poor. For *Lebanon* is the council of the community, and *the beasts* are the simple ones of Judah, the doers of the law. God will condemn him to destruction even as he plotted to destroy the poor. And as for the words, *for the blood of a city and violence to the land*, the *city* is to be interpreted as Jerusalem, in which the Wicked Priest wrought abominable works and defiled the sanctuary of God; and *violence to the land* refers to the cities of Judah, where he plundered the wealth of the poor."

So the Wicked Priest did not even spare the poor in his greed for gain. But the commentator is thinking of a particular class of poor—his own community. For the members of the Qumran community liked to speak of themselves as "the poor," taking their cue from various Old Testament passages where "poor" and "pious" are practically synonymous. It may be, then, that one of the forms of persecution which the Teacher of Righteousness and his followers had to endure at the hands of the Wicked Priest was the confiscation of their property.

But all this ill-gotten gain would bring no good to those who laid their hands on it. The prophet had said: "Because you have plundered many nations, all the remnant of the peoples shall plunder you" (Hab. 2: 8). And this, according to the commentator, refers to "the last priests of Jerusalem, who piled up wealth and unjust gain from the plunder of the peoples, but in the last days their wealth, with their plunder, will be given into the hand of the arny of the Kitti'im, for they are *the remnant of the peoples.*"

These references to the Wicked Priest have been quoted in some detail, because they help us to come to certain conclusions about his place in history. As the Jerusalem priesthood, in any official and executive capacity, came to an end with the destruction of the temple in A.D. 70, we naturally think of him as flourishing before that date. Since he is said to have "ruled in Israel" we may perhaps think of him as a member of the Hasmonean dynasty of priest-kings, who governed Judæa for some eighty years before the Roman conquest in 63 B.C. In that case there is one figure who has special claims to be considered as the Wicked Priest. That is Alexander Jannaeus, who became king and high priest of the Jews in 103 B.C., and held office until 76 B.C. He was notoriously a persecutor of certain pious groups in Judæa, particularly of those who considered either his high priesthood or his ritual procedure irregular; he was, moreover, a military adventurer with an insatiable lust for conquest, and in the course of his campaigns he reduced many Gentile cities on the Palestinian seaboard and in Transjordan and added them to his kingdom, enriching himself with their plunder. When he died, his widow, Salome Alexandra, succeeded to the civil sovereignty, and their elder son, Hyrcanus II, became high priest. The years following Salome Alexandra's death in 67 B.C. were marked by civil war between the partisans of Hyrcanus and his ambitious younger brother, Aristobulus II; but in 63 B.C. the Romans intervened and not only imposed peace on the warring factions but exacted a heavy tribute from the Jewish state. This might well be viewed as at least a

E.I.F.E. College Library
1100 Glendale Blvd.
Los Angeles 26, Calif.

beginning of the fulfilment of the commentator's prediction that the wealth and plunder of the last priests of Jerusalem would be given into the hand of the army of the Kitti'im.

It might be urged against the identification of Alexander Jannaeus with the Wicked Priest that he did not meet his death at the hands of his enemies, and that they did not inflict torments "upon his body of flesh." We must remember that persecuted communities have been prone to exaggerate the torments suffered by their persecutors, and to ascribe these to the avenging wrath of heaven. But Alexander Jannaeus did on more than one occasion suffer crushing defeats at the hand of his enemies. In 100 B.C. he had an army annihilated and nearly lost his kingdom to the Egyptians; in 94 B.C. another army of his was ambushed and wiped out by Arabians in Transjordan and he escaped with his bare life; this was followed by a revolt on the part of many of his Jewish subjects in which he was again beaten and forced to seek refuge in the mountains (88 B.C.). But what of the "judgments of wickedness," the "horrors of sore diseases," the "vengeance upon his body of flesh" with which he was smitten? The commentator does not say (so far as we can make out) that these were tortures inflicted upon him by human enemies into whose hands he had fallen. But the closing years of his life were marked by a distressing bodily ailment—a quartan ague, Josephus tells us—and when our commentator says of the Wicked Priest that "they" smote him with judgments of wickedness and wrought horrors of sore diseases upon him, and vengeance upon his body of flesh, it is natural to infer that "they," according to a well-known Hebraic idiom, refers to the supernatural executors of divine judgment.[1] Josephus tells us, moreover, that Alexander's illness was the result of hard drinking; and this chimes in with the commentator's statement that the Wicked Priest "walked in the ways of drunkenness to quench his thirst."

If the secession of the Qumran community is to be dated in Alexander's reign, it may be set in the context of other disputes which set that king at loggerheads with many of his subjects.

One story relates how at the Feast of Tabernacles, where he was officiating as high priest, he mismanaged the ceremony of the

[1] A good example of this idiom appears in our Lord's parable of the rich fool (Luke 12: 16–21); the divine message to him runs literally thus: "Fool! This night *they are requiring* your soul from you . . ."

water-pouring with such deliberate disregard of what the people counted the proper ritual that the spectators pelted him with citrons (which they held in their hands as part of the requirements of the occasion). In his fury he sent soldiers among them, and a large number were slaughtered.[1]

It was in his reign that the breach between his dynasty and the Pharisees became complete; and the circumstances which so alienated the Pharisees would certainly alienate the disciples of the Teacher of Righteousness as well. Echoes of the bitterness of the conflict between Alexander and the Pharisees may be heard in various places throughout the rabbinical literature of later days: on several occasions reference is made in this literature to the time "when King Jannaeus put the rabbis to death."

The Talmud[2] has preserved the record of a feast in celebration of a victorious campaign in Transjordan, to which the king invited all the wise men of Israel. At this feast "there was a man, frivolous, evil-hearted and worthless, named Eleazar Ben-Po'irah," who told the king that the hearts of the Pharisees were disaffected towards him. To prove his charge, he urged the king to put on the high-priestly turban, with its plate of gold bearing the inscription: "Holy to the LORD." It was incumbent upon those who were present to rise as a token of reverence when the high priest put on this mitre. But one of the wise men present (Judah Ben-Gedidiah by name) exhorted the king to content himself with the royal crown, and leave the priestly crown to the seed of Aaron. There was an implied insult in this exhortation which had already estranged Alexander's father, John Hyrcanus, from the Pharisees. For it was said by some that the legitimacy of John's birth was in doubt on the ground that his mother, the wife of Simon Maccabaeus, had been for some time a prisoner of war in the hands of the Seleucid authorities. They therefore doubted whether John was truly the son of Simon and consequently an inheritor of the priestly seed of Aaron. John's legitimacy, however, was vindicated after legal inquiry, but some of the sages would not be satisfied, and now the matter was raised again by way of an objection to the tenure of the high-priesthood

[1] This story is reconstructed by piecing together an incident narrated by Josephus in his *Antiquities* (xiii. 13. 5) and one preserved in the Babylonian Talmud, tractate *Sukkah* (48*b*).

[2] In the tractate *Qiddushin* (66*a*).

by his son Alexander. The other wise men who were present at the feast appear to have preserved a discreet silence when their colleague spoke so undiplomatically. But the king asked Eleazar Ben-Po'irah what treatment they deserved, and Eleazar answered: "If you will take my advice, trample them down." Accordingly, says the Talmudic narrative, all the wise men of Israel were massacred, except Simeon Ben-Shetach (brother of Queen Salome Alexandra), who was hidden by his sister and restored the sacred law to its former glory after Alexander's death.

The Teacher of Righteousness and his disciples were not Pharisees in the usual sense of the term. Their interpretation of the law and their discipline were severer than those of the Pharisees, but we may be sure that any objection which the Pharisees felt to the tenure of the high-priesthood by the Hasmoneans would be felt more keenly and expressed more vigorously by the men of Qumran. An element of legend is plainly to be seen in the Talmudic narrative, and it confuses two or three quite distinct incidents. But there is a sound historical core, and it is possible that the Teacher's withdrawal to the wilderness of Judah with his followers was connected with Alexander's attack on the rabbis.

One might even toy with the idea of linking the feast given by Alexander to the rabbis with the occasion referred to by the Habakkuk commentator in his note on Hab. 1: 13 ("why dost thou look on faithless men, and art silent when the wicked swallows up the man more righteous than he?"). "The interpretation of this," says the commentator, "concerns the house of Absalom and the men of their council who kept silence when the Teacher of Righteousness was rebuked, and did not come to his aid against the Man of Falsehood, who rejected the law in the midst of all their congregation."

Was the Teacher of Righteousness Judah Ben-Gedidiah?[1] One dare not express this idea otherwise than in the form of a question, because nothing is known about Judah which could justify a more positive expression of opinion.

And who was the Man of Falsehood? He may conceivably have been the Wicked Priest himself, or else someone, like Eleazar

[1] This identification was suggested by W. H. Brownlee in an article, "The Historical Allusions of the Dead Sea Habakkuk Midrash," in the *Bulletin of the American Schools of Oriental Research*, No. 126 (April, 1952), pp. 10 ff.

Ben-Po'irah, who aided and abetted him. But from allusions elsewhere in the Zadokite and Qumran writings it seems that he was the leader of a rival religious movement, which (in the eyes of the Teacher of Righteousness and his followers) "led the simple astray." The identification of this rival movement must be a matter for further study; it is worth considering whether the reference may not be to Simeon Ben-Shetach and the Pharisees who followed him.

As for the men of the "house of Absalom," who kept silence when they ought to have spoken out in defence of the Teacher of Righteousness, their identity remains to be determined. Some scholars have pointed out that Alexander Jannaeus had a younger brother named Absalom (whose daughter married Alexander's younger son Aristobulus). But the commentator may have given the name "house of Absalom" to some group of people because he detected a resemblance between their conduct and that of Absalom, the handsome son of King David who rebelled against his father.

Our identification of the Wicked Priest with Alexander Jannaeus can be no more than tentative; it must be submitted to constant re-examination as further evidence comes to light. But at the time of writing, no other historical figure seems to satisfy so many of the conditions as does Alexander.

This identification, however, does not make it much easier to give a name to the Teacher of Righteousness, although it does provide him with a historical setting. Some have thought of an Essene named Judah, who figures in an incident at the Hasmonean court only a month or two before Alexander's accession to the throne; others have thought of a pious Jew named Onias,[1] who was stoned to death by the partisans of Hyrcanus II shortly before the Roman conquest in 63 B.C. But nothing that is related of either of these good men bears any relation to the activities of the Teacher of Righteousness, as these can be reconstructed from the Zadokite and Qumran texts.

As the character of the Teacher has been studied with increasing

[1] He was known as Onias the rain-maker because of the efficacy of his prayers for rain. But whereas Josephus tells how he was stoned to death for refusing to pray for rain in order to secure military advantage for Hyrcanus's forces against those of his brother Aristobulus, the Talmud tells how he experienced a Rip Van Winkle sleep of seventy years' duration, and died of grief soon after he woke up because no one recognized him.

interest and thoroughness during recent years, he has inevitably been compared with the Founder of Christianity. One Cambridge scholar, indeed (Dr. J. L. Teicher), has gone so far as to identify them. Others have been content with pointing out (and at times exaggerating) the features in which the Teacher appears to have anticipated Jesus. They were both founders of new communities which sprang from the commonwealth of Israel. They both laid down the outlines of a creative method of Biblical interpretation which largely served as the groundwork for their followers' theological beliefs and directed their course of action. They were both venerated by their followers; if the Qumran sect believed that the way to receive a verdict of acquittal in the divine court was to have faith in the Teacher of Righteousness, the New Testament proclaims that God justifies the man who has faith in Jesus; and in both cases Old Testament authority for this tenet was found in the words: "The just shall live by (his) faith" (Hab. 2: 4). There is this difference, however, that faith in the Teacher of Righteousness implied mainly faith in his teaching, whereas saving faith in Jesus, according to the New Testament, includes in addition personal commitment to Him as Lord and Redeemer. To His first followers Jesus was the promised Messiah; there is no evidence, on the other hand, that the Teacher of Righteousness ever claimed that dignity for himself or received it from his followers. His death, in fact, preceded the expected advent of the Messiah or Messiahs by some years; at best, therefore, he was but a precursor of the Messiah, as John the Baptist was. Indeed, he was identified with John the Baptist by the late Dr. Robert Eisler, but this identification is untenable. For (among other things) it was not at the hands of a wicked priest that John the Baptist suffered, but at the hands of Herod Antipas and his wife Herodias.

Nothing is known thus far about the manner of the Teacher's death. Attempts to show that it was a remarkable anticipation of the death of Jesus have not been successful. Professor Dupont-Sommer maintains that the horrors which were perpetrated on the Wicked Priest's "body of flesh," according to the Habakkuk commentary, were perpetrated on the Teacher, not on the Wicked Priest;[1] but this is an unnatural reading of the commentator's language. He further holds that the passage

[1] *The Dead Sea Scrolls*, p. 34.

which tells how the Wicked Priest burst upon the Teacher and his followers in their hiding-place "to swallow them up" on the day of atonement refers to an epiphany of the martyred Teacher which burst upon the Wicked Priest and his followers on the day of atonement in 63 B.C.—the very day which witnessed the storming of the temple area in Jerusalem by Pompey's forces.[1] But this too is a strained interpretation of the text.

Mr. J. M. Allegro, who also defends the view that the Teacher was violently put to death, mentions a fragment of a commentary on the Book of Nahum, found in Cave 4, which supports the dating of the community's foundation in the time of Alexander Jannaeus by certain historical allusions, and also refers to the practice of "hanging men up alive"—which may reasonably be understood to mean crucifixion.[2] Mr. Allegro then argues that, if crucifixion is mentioned in a Qumran commentary, it must have had some special significance for the sect. Now the Teacher of Righteousness opposed Alexander (if he is to be identified with the Wicked Priest), and since Alexander is known to have crucified men who rebelled against him, it is inferred that the Teacher may have suffered this fate.

There is nothing in the passage specified by Mr. Allegro to suggest that the Teacher was one of those "hung up alive." And the rebels whom Alexander crucified were men who had organized a military revolt against him and called in a foreign army to help to overthrow him. The revolt did nearly succeed, but when Alexander at last was able to crush it, he took a ghastly revenge on those of its leaders on whom he could lay hands. "As he feasted with his concubines in the sight of all the city," says Josephus, "he ordered about eight hundred of them to be crucified, and while they were still living ordered the throats of their wives and children to be cut before their eyes." The lesson was not lost on those of his opponents who were still at large. About eight thousand of them fled by night, and remained in exile during the remainder of his reign. This supreme barbarity might well be mentioned by any writer who wished to put Alexander's

[1] Op. cit., pp. 27 f., 44. It is, however, not at all certain that the temple area was taken on the day of atonement.

[2] See his article "Further Light on the History of the Qumran Sect" in the *Journal of Biblical Literature* 75 (1956), pp. 89 ff., and his Pelican Book, *The Dead Sea Scrolls* (1956), pp. 98 ff.

impiety on permanent record, without our being forced to the conclusion that the Teacher of Righteousness was one of those crucified by him.

As has been said, we simply do not know how the Teacher met his death. Nor is there any evidence that his followers attached atoning value to his death, as the early Christians did to the death of Jesus, when (following His own example) they interpreted the significance of His passion in terms of the suffering Servant of Isa. 53. The Qumran covenanters did not ignore Isa. 53, but (so far as we can tell) they did not view it as being fulfilled in the experience of the Teacher of Righteousness alone, or in that of any other individual.

When the Teacher of Righteousness died, the momentous events which his ministry was expected to usher in had not even begun to take place. It may well be that his followers for this reason conceived the belief that he would rise again in the latter days to continue the work which his death had interrupted, until the messianic age had fully come. But even if he was expected to have such a special resurrection, before the general resurrection of the righteous, there is no evidence that he did rise from the dead, or that anyone ever thought he had done so.[1]

[1] Professor H. H. Rowley has argued for the identification of the Teacher of Righteousness with Onias III, the last legitimate high priest of the house of Zadok, who was deposed in 175 B.C. The Wicked Priest would then be Menelaus, who usurped the sacred office and procured the assassination of Onias III in 171 B.C.; the Man of Falsehood is further identified with Antiochus Epiphanes and the house of Absalom with the Jewish family of the Tobiads, whose unedifying history is recorded by Josephus. Professor Rowley's judgment is always so sound that any view which he espouses deserves the most careful consideration. His arguments are set forth in *The Zadokite Fragments and the Dead Sea Scrolls*, pp. 62 ff. A similar view is defended by the Abbé A. Michel in *Le Maître de Justice* (1954).

CHAPTER IX

THE QUMRAN COMMUNITY

AN attempt can now be made to give a provisional outline of the history and character of the Qumran community. There are many gaps to be filled in, and it may be that some parts of our outline will be shown, in the light of further evidence and study, to be based on misinterpretations of the data at present available. But this is the story to which the documentary and archaeological findings seem to point.

Since the time of Alexander the Great (332 B.C.) Judæa had been under the control of Macedonian dynasties. From 312 to 198 B.C. the Ptolemaic dynasty of Egypt dominated the country; in the latter year the Ptolemies lost Judæa to the Seleucid dynasty whose capital was Antioch in Syria. But the Jews of Judæa continued to enjoy the liberal measure of home rule, under the hereditary high priests of the house of Zadok, that had been theirs under the Persian Empire. Nevertheless, the influence of Greek life and thought was very powerful, and many of the pious Jews feared that their nation's distinctive way of life, based on the law of God, would go down before the encroachments of Hellenism. They therefore banded themselves together to maintain the faith and practice of their fathers, to resist the insidious approaches of paganism, and to influence others by their example and teaching. They were known as the *hasidim*—the "pious people." Among them were some who figure in the Book of Daniel as the *maskilim*—a term which is variously translated "the wise" and "the teachers" (and it is not of great moment which of the two renderings is adopted, because those men both cultivated true wisdom themselves and taught it to their fellows).

The relative peace which the people of Judæa had enjoyed under their Hellenistic overlords began to be disturbed shortly after Antiochus IV (Epiphanes) ascended the Seleucid throne in 175 B.C. Early in his reign he interfered with the succession to the high-priesthood, and in 171 B.C. replaced the Zadokite dynasty by an upstart high priest, Menelaus, who promised to press on energetically with the policy of Hellenization in Judæa. In the following years the king was ill-advised enough to make further attacks on the Jewish way of life. At last, in 167 B.C., the distinctive features of the Jewish religion (such as circumcision and the keeping of the sabbath day) were proscribed, the sacred books of the law and the prophets were seized and destroyed, participation in pagan ceremonies was enforced throughout Judæa, and at the end of that year the temple in Jerusalem was consecrated to the worship of a pagan deity. This was the deity whose name was slightly altered by the scandalized Jews to a form which the English Bible translates as "the abomination of desolation"—or, as Dr. Moffatt rendered it, "the appalling horror."

Naturally, the pious members of the community recognized in this policy a challenge which must be resisted to the death, and great numbers of them died for their faith. In the words of Daniel, "the people who know their God shall stand firm and take action; and those among the people who are wise (the *maskilim*) shall make many understand, though they shall fall by sword and flame, by captivity and plunder, for some days" (Dan. 11: 32, 33). But other members of the nation were not content with a passive resistance. These found leaders in an aged priest named Mattathias and his five sons (Judas Maccabaeus and his brothers), who took up arms against the oppressor and won a series of striking guerrilla victories against his forces. For a time the *hasidim* made common cause with this insurgent movement. So successful was the resistance that within three years the king and his advisers realized the folly of their action. The ban on the Jewish religion was rescinded, and exactly three years after the inauguration of the pagan cult in the Jerusalem temple, the holy place was occupied by Judas Maccabaeus and his followers, solemnly cleansed of the idolatrous pollution, and rededicated to the worship of the God of Israel.

But the situation could not simply revert to what it had been at the beginning of the reign of Antiochus IV. Judas and his men had won religious freedom by force of arms; might they not win full political independence in the same way? So they continued the struggle, and were greatly helped by increasing civil strife in the Seleucid kingdom, in the course of which one rival for the imperial throne after another tried to enlist the aid of the seasoned guerrilla force which Judas and his brothers had built up. At last, in 142 B.C., the last trace of Gentile domination was expelled from Judæa and an independent Jewish state was proclaimed, with Simon, the last survivor of the Maccabaean brothers (although he was the oldest of them), as head of the state. This meant that he was not only chief civil ruler and military leader, but high priest as well. The Hasmonean family, to which he belonged, was a priestly family indeed, but many of the *hasidim* had come to look with growing disfavour on its self-regarding ambition, and considered that its assumption of the high-priesthood was an act of usurpation. Their relations with the Hasmonean dynasty became increasingly strained in the reign of Simon's son John Hyrcanus (135–104 B.C.), and a complete breach followed soon after the accession of Alexander Jannaeus (103 B.C.). Many of the *hasidim* organized themselves as the party of the Pharisees, but one group found a leader in the Teacher of Righteousness. Under his leadership they withdrew to the wilderness of Judæa, and organized themselves as a religious community with its headquarters at Qumran. For this withdrawal they found prophetic authority in the words of Isa. 40: 3:

> In the wilderness prepare ye the way of the LORD;
> Make straight in the desert a highway for our God.

The Teacher of Righteousness enabled them to interpret the writings of the prophets in such a way as to show them the part which they had to play in the last days, which he believed were swiftly approaching. If the nation of Israel as a whole was unfit to accomplish the purpose of God, it was their privilege to act as the faithful remnant of the nation. So they were organized as a miniature Israel, comprising priests, Levites and commoners, living in "camps" after the pattern of Israel during the wilderness wanderings in the time of Moses. They bound themselves by a "new covenant" to engage in the careful study and practice of the law of God against the dawning of the new age. In fact, their faithfulness, they believed, would bring in everlasting righteousness the more speedily. They called themselves by such various titles as *maskilim*, saints (*hasidim*) of the Most High, the holy people of the covenant, the poor of the flock, the sons of light, the men of truth, the elect of God, the community of Israel and Aaron.

L.I.F.E. College Libr
1100 Glendale
Los Angeles, Calif. 90026

They described themselves as "volunteers for holiness"; they were men who willingly offered themselves for a highly responsible and honourable ministry. Their interpretation of the law was exceedingly strict—stricter than the Pharisaic "tradition of the elders" which incurred the criticism of Jesus in His day. They attached great importance to ritual purification by bathing in water, but they insisted that outward cleansing was useless if it was not accompanied by inward purity of heart. The cleansing which they sought, in fact, was that sprinkling with clean water, that outpouring of a new spirit, that bestowal of an obedient heart, which God promises to His people in Ezek. 36: 25 ff. They looked forward to a new Jerusalem and a new temple, where acceptable sacrifices would be offered up by a worthy priesthood. But most striking of all their beliefs is the conception of their duty as the making of expiation for their fellow-Israelites. Their devotion to the divine law, their endurance of suffering, their submission to severe discipline—all this, they hoped and believed, would be accepted by God as an atonement for the sins of the nation which had gone so far astray from the path of His will. Their duty, as they conceived it, was nothing less than the fulfilment of the rôle appointed for the obedient and suffering Servant of the Lord in Isa. 52: 13–53: 12. Did God say through the prophet: "By his knowledge shall the righteous one, my servant, make many to be accounted righteous; and he shall bear their iniquities"? Then, with God's help, they would make this their aim. And when the detailed prescriptions of their Rule were carried out "to establish a holy spirit for eternal truth, to make propitiation for the guilt of rebellion and for sinful faithlessness, and to obtain favour for the land apart from the flesh of burnt-offerings and the fat of sacrifice; then [said they] the oblation of the lips according to judgment shall be as a sweet savour of righteousness, and the perfectness of one's way as an acceptable freewill offering."

Thanks to the instruction of the Teacher of Righteousness, who had marked out the path of holiness for them and shown them how they might serve the divine purpose in the end-time, they set themselves by these means to save themselves and their less enlightened brethren. But propitiation was not the only task which they had to undertake; when the hour struck, they would be called upon to execute the work of judgment as well.

This work of judgment would be promoted by the coming war against the sons of darkness, but the guilty leaders in Israel would also reap the due reward of their deeds. For the rank and file who had been led astray there would be mercy through the community's work of propitiation; but for those who had deliberately led them astray the day of vengeance lay ahead. "By the hand of His elect God will judge all the nations; and by their rebuke those who have kept His commandments in the time of their distress will condemn all the wicked of His people."

There was no inconsistency between their propitiatory work and the execution of judgment upon the ungodly; the community was to realize not only the figure of the Servant of the Lord who makes many to be accounted righteous, but also the figure of that "one like a son of man" who, in Daniel's night vision, receives from the Ancient of Days authority to execute judgment and wield eternal and universal dominion (Dan. 7: 13 f., 22).

Their insight into the essential identity of these two prophetic figures is specially noteworthy. The two figures, as is well known, are fused in the teaching of Jesus, who derived His chosen title as Son of Man from Dan. 7: 13, but interpreted it as pointing not only to the executor of divine judgment but also to the Isaianic Servant enduring affliction for the sins of others. If He spoke of the Son of Man "sitting at the right hand of Power, and coming with the clouds of heaven" (Mark 14: 62), He also emphasized repeatedly that the Son of Man must "suffer many things and be treated with contempt" (Mark 9: 13).

What is not so well known is that the two figures—the Servant of the Lord and the Son of Man—were from the first *intended* to be identical; that the one whom Daniel saw in his vision was the Isaianic Servant under another guise. As close students of the visions of Daniel, as heirs of those *maskilim* whose aim (according to Dan. 12: 3) was to "turn many to righteousness," the Qumran community recognized this. Their purpose to fulfil this twofold rôle was noble indeed, even if they failed to achieve it.

When we consider the solemn responsibility to which these "sons of the covenant" dedicated themselves, we may understand why they thought it necessary to bind themselves by such a strict discipline. Only by perfect righteousness could their task of vicarious expiation be accomplished.

The true *maskil* was instructed to teach his fellows the true knowledge of God. From the emphasis on "knowledge" in several of the community documents it has been inferred by some students that the *maskilim* and their pupils pursued a form of gnosticism. That is a truism, if we understand the term *gnosis* ("knowledge") in its general sense, but it is also misleading, because by gnosticism is usually meant the pursuit of a special conception of *gnosis* which is not found in the Qumran documents. We shall look in vain here for that *gnosis* which enables the soul to liberate itself progressively from its imprisonment in matter by ascending through the spheres to the upper realm of spirit. The knowledge cultivated at Qumran was the knowledge recommended in the Old Testament Wisdom books, which finds its source in the fear of God. One aspect of this knowledge, however, which is specially emphasized is the knowledge of the mysteries of the divine purpose, to be unfolded in full at the end of the present world-order. One stage of this knowledge was imparted by God to His servants the prophets, but a further stage was reserved for the Teacher of Righteousness and his disciples, who were initiated into the mystery of the time when God would fulfil the things revealed to the prophets. "None of the wicked shall understand; but those who are wise (the *maskilim*) shall understand" (Dan. 12: 10). The prophets (as the apostle Peter was to say at a later date) might inquire and search diligently concerning the person or time intended by the Spirit by whose power they spoke; but these *maskilim* believed they had mastered the secret which eluded the prophets.

Another feature of gnosticism which has been detected in the Qumran writings is dualism. In the *Rule of the Community* two spirits are said to dominate human life between them—the spirit of truth and the spirit of error. "In the abode of light are the origins of truth, and in the spring of darkness are the origins of error. In the hand of the prince of lights is dominion over all the sons of righteousness, and they walk in the ways of light. And in the hand of the angel of darkness is all the dominion of the sons of error, and they walk in the ways of darkness." Certainly this may be called dualism, but it is a dualism brought into subjection to the Biblical doctrine of God the Creator, who forms light and creates darkness (Isa. 45: 7). For both these spirits are creatures of the one God, together with everything else that exists. "From the God of knowledge is everything that is and that is to be; even before they existed, He established all their design." This is emphasized more than once in words practically identical with the Fourth Evangelist's affirmation about the Divine Logos: "All things were made through him, and without him was not anything made that was made" (John 1: 3).

The organization of the community was hierarchical: there were priests (called variously "sons of Aaron" or "sons of Zadok"), Levites, elders, and the rank and file. It was governed by a supreme council consisting of twelve laymen and three priests. Certain important matters were to be decided by lot, which was cast under the direction of the sons of Aaron. This preserved the tradition of earlier days in Israel when the will of God was ascertained by the priests by means of the sacred lot, the Urim and Thummim.

From time to time a general assembly of the community was held—"the session of the many,"[1] as it was called. Rules of precedence were laid down with regard to the taking of their seats —first the priests, then the elders, then the rest of the people, each in his position—and standing orders for the conduct of the meeting were strictly enforced. Anyone who wished to speak had to stand up and say: "I have a word to speak to the many." If he received permission from the leaders, he might speak. And while he was speaking no other member might interrupt him. Such unseemly behaviour as speaking foolishly, laughing out loud, sleeping while the session was in progress, or leaving the room too often without due cause, received appropriate punishment. Punishment commonly took the form of expulsion for a set period from the purificatory rites and the communal meal, or the reduction of a man's rations for a specified time.

Over each of the camps into which the community was divided there was an inspector, and over them all a chief inspector, to see that discipline was maintained.

One of the duties of this chief inspector was to examine candidates for admission to the community, to see if their motives and their lives were pure and if they understood what they were doing. Those who passed this first examination had then to appear before the general assembly of "the many" and be accepted or refused by them. If they were accepted, they had to

[1] Some render this expression "the session of the great ones." But "the session of the many" seems definitely preferable.

pass through two stages of initiation, each of them lasting one year, before they were enrolled as full members. During the first year they retained their private property; during the second year it was deposited with the community treasurer, but not until he became a full member at the beginning of the third year was it merged with the common fund. A stern penalty was imposed on a member who "knowingly deceived in regard to property" —but not so stern as the judgment which overtook Ananias and Sapphira when they committed this offence in the early days of the Jerusalem church.

When a man was admitted to the covenanted community, he had to swear a solemn vow to return to the law of Moses with all his heart and shun all contact with ungodly men. While he was doing so, the priests recited blessings on those who set their hearts to walk in God's ways, and the Levites recited the curses which would descend on those who committed apostasy.

Women as well as men might be admitted to the community, and marriage and family life were not discouraged. This is evident enough from some of the relevant documents, and is borne out by the evidence of the cemetery on the east of Khirbet Qumran, where women as well as men were buried.

The archaeological evidence of the great baptisteries uncovered at Khirbet Qumran agrees with the emphasis placed on ritual cleansing in water in the *Rule of the Community*. We gather that this cleansing was not merely an initiatory rite, but one performed frequently. But it is made abundantly plain that ritual washing alone had no efficacy if a man's heart was not right with God. The washing of the body was religiously acceptable only if it was the outward sign of a purified and humble soul within. So characteristic, moreover, do these washings appear to have been that the community fellowship is commonly designated as "the purity of the many."

Communal meals, communal worship and communal consultation were regular features of the community. These communal activities, however, did not always involve the coming together of the whole community; they could be carried out wherever ten members were gathered together, provided that one of the ten was a priest. It was necessary, for example, that when they met for a communal meal, whether as a group of ten or as a larger number, the priest should say grace before they partook of bread or wine. And where there was such a group of ten, it had to be arranged that one of them was always engaged in the study and exposition of the holy law. This seems to have been arranged by relays, so that the study and exposition were carried on continuously. The night was divided into three watches, and during each watch one-third of the membership kept awake to listen to the reading and exposition, and to voice the appointed blessings.

While Khirbet Qumran was their headquarters, they would not all live there; the hundreds of caves in the district no doubt served as "cells" for many of them.

Those who were finally admitted as full members of the community handed over their property (as we have seen) to the common stock, which was administered by the community treasurer in accordance with the direction of the council. They appear to have done the same with the wages or other income which they acquired during their membership of the community. For it is plain that they did not shirk manual labour, and were willing to do menial service for the ungodly, showing them humble deference outwardly, while cherishing very different sentiments towards them at heart. In an important article on "The Economic Basis of the Qumran Community"[1] Professor William R. Farmer of Drew University, Madison (N.J.), points out the importance of the questions: "How could such an established community have maintained itself in so desolate an environment? How did these people subsist? How did they obtain food, clothing, writing material, cooking utensils, etc., which were necessary for their community life?" He then considers the various kinds of work that were available to them, and pays special attention to work connected with the products of the Dead Sea, work connected with the neighbouring oasis of Ain Feshkha, and work which might have been carried on within the community headquarters. He shows how they could have worked as agriculturalists, herdsmen, bee-keepers, and so forth, and could have sold various kinds of produce and manufactured articles. Nor need we suppose that all the members spent all the time at Qumran. By working in more populated parts of Judæa, and handing over to the community all their earnings apart from their bare subsistence requirements, many of them could have contributed to the maintenance of community life.

[1] In the *Theologische Zeitschrift*, July–August, 1955, pp. 295 ff.

Thus, then, they pursued their chosen course of plain living and high thinking. The Roman occupation of Judæa in 63 B.C. filled them with hope that the hour of fulfilment, for which they so earnestly looked, was about to strike. But the expected signal was continually deferred. Early in the reign of Herod the Great (37–4 B.C.), for reasons which call for further investigation, they abandoned Khirbet Qumran and betook themselves perhaps to the neighbourhood of Damascus.[1] During their absence considerable damage was done to their headquarters by the earthquake of 31 B.C. But when they heard of Herod's death, they returned, and the fact that "Archelaus reigned over Judæa in place of his father Herod" did not deter them, as it did the holy family, from settling down once more in Judæa. They rebuilt and reinforced Khirbet Qumran, and continued the way of life which they had followed before their temporary exile.

But the time of the end was still delayed. Not far from their headquarters a man of priestly birth, one John the son of Zechariah (who may have been known to many of them), began to proclaim a baptism of repentance for the forgiveness of sins around A.D. 27, in preparation for the imminent advent of "The Coming One" who was to carry out a purifying work of judgment. But John's ministry does not appear to have influenced the men of Qumran. Not long afterwards another preacher in Galilee, farther north, proclaimed that the appointed time had fully come and that the kingdom of God had drawn near, and called on the people to repent and believe in this good news. But even this ministry, with its sequel on a cross at Jerusalem, caused little if any repercussion at Qumran. They continued to wait.

There were, however, other men in Israel who did not believe in waiting, but in launching an attack on the occupying power and winning the divine kingdom by force. Many of their attempts were crushed, but one which was made in A.D. 66 was attended by an astonishing degree of initial success. Many Jews thought that the Roman grip on their land was broken. What the Qumran community thought, as they saw these "men of violence" take the field against the sons of darkness, we can only guess. But it meant the end of their life and their hopes in the form which they had taken since the days of the Teacher of Righteousness.

[1] This depends on our interpretation of certain references in the Zadokite work (see p. 32, n. 1).

For the Romans were not daunted by initial reverses. In May of A.D. 68 Vespasian, commander of the Roman forces charged with putting down the Jewish revolt, advanced from the north upon Jericho, and took it easily (the inhabitants having fled at his approach). He then sent the tenth legion against Jerusalem, leaving a garrison in Jericho. Since the coin record at Khirbet Qumran, so far as its occupation by the community is concerned, comes to an end in A.D. 68, it is not unreasonable to conclude that the community abandoned its headquarters at the approach of the Romans. But first they stored the community library in the caves near their settlement, wrapping the scrolls carefully in linen and placing them in jars of a suitable shape and size. No doubt they hoped that more peaceful conditions would be restored in due course and that they would be able to return to Qumran, retrieve their books, and resume their community life. But these hopes were not to be realized. They never returned. As for their precious books, it may be that once or twice, in the course of the centuries, some people stumbled upon one or another of the caves in which they were hidden. It may even be that the recovery of some of these documents helped to bring about a reformation movement in the Judaism of the eighth century which persisted here and there until our own day. But for the most part the books lay forgotten in the caves, slowly disintegrating with the passage of time, until their fragmentary remains were recently brought to light in such an unexpected fashion.

Note on Earlier Manuscript Discoveries

It is a matter of very great interest that other manuscript discoveries in Palestine (some of them in the region with which we are specially concerned) have been reported from earlier days.

For example, somewhere about A.D. 217 the illustrious Christian scholar Origen found some Hebrew and Greek books, including a Greek version of the Old Testament Psalms (different from the Septuagint version) "in a jar near Jericho." At the time when Cave 1 at Qumran was the only one known to contain manuscripts, some people thought that Origen's jar of scrolls must have come from it; it was even incautiously suggested that a Roman lamp and cooking-pot found in the cave might have been left by him! The Greek version of the Psalms which he found was incorporated in his great critical edition of the Bible called the Hexapla.

Many centuries after Origen's time, about the year 800, we have an account of the discovery of a cave in the Dead Sea region containing manuscripts of Old Testament books and other Hebrew works. This discovery is mentioned in a letter written by Timotheus, Patriarch of the Nestorian Christians, to Sergius, Metropolitan Bishop of Elam. (Like the discovery in 1947, this one was made by accident; a Bedouin shepherd went in search of his dog, who had followed a sheep through a hole and did not come out again.)

A century or two later we have further evidence (probably relating to the discovery mentioned by Timotheus) from Qirqisani, a tenth-century writer who belonged to the Jewish sect of the Qaraites. The Qaraites, who arose in the eighth century A.D. (and survived until Hitler wiped out their last remnants in the Crimea during the Second World War), rejected the rabbinical traditions preserved in the Talmud and claimed to base their beliefs and practices directly on the written text of the Hebrew Bible.

Qirqisani, in an account of various Jewish sects, makes reference to one which he calls the "Cave Sect" because their literature was discovered in a cave. He quotes an earlier writer, David Ibn-Merwan, as his authority for this reference. A later writer named Al-Biruni also refers to the "Cave Sect," giving a ninth-century author as his authority. Yet another reference to the "Cave Sect" appears in the works of Shahrastani, who lived in the eleventh and twelfth centuries. According to him, this sect flourished four hundred years before the Alexandrian heresiarch Arius. As Arius was specially prominent at the time of the Council of Nicaea (A.D. 325), this indication of time (if we can place any reliance on it) points to the first century B.C. as the period of the "Cave Sect." Perhaps Qirqisani implies a similar dating for them, if there is any chronological significance in the fact that he mentions them between the Sadducees (who first appear towards the end of the second century B.C.) and the followers of Jesus of Nazareth (who arose, of course, in the first century A.D.).

It looks as if this "Cave Sect" might be identical with our Qumran community, the more so as Qirqisani tells us that it followed a different calendar from the ordinary one.

It looks, moreover, as if Qirqisani was not the only Qaraite Jew to be interested in the "Cave Sect" and its literature. There are some quite interesting points of contact between the Qumran texts and Qaraite doctrine (so much so that one eminent Jewish scholar in this country, Dr. P. R. Weis, has made the archaeologically impossible suggestion that the Qumran texts reflect Qaraite influence). A *prima facie* case can be made out for the view that the early development of Qaraite doctrine was considerably indebted to the chance discovery of Qumran texts just about the time when the Qaraite movement originated. It is worth mentioning that it is apparently to Qaraite scribes that we owe the two fragmentary copies of the Zadokite work which lay concealed for so many centuries in the Cairo genizah. Was this one of the works discovered among the literature of the "Cave Sect" in the eighth century? It seems highly probable.

CHAPTER X

QUMRAN AND THE ESSENES

INEVITABLY we ask if there is any group of pious Jews mentioned in contemporary literature with which the community of Qumran might be identified. And, almost as inevitably, we are reminded of the people called the Essenes, concerning whom a considerable body of information is provided for us by three writers of the first century A.D. Two of these writers are Jews who wrote in Greek—the Alexandrian Philo and the Palestinian Josephus—and the other is a Roman, the elder Pliny.

Pliny's account is worth quoting in full. It comes in the fifth book of his *Natural History* and was written between A.D. 73 (the year of the reduction of Masada) and 79 (the year of Pliny's death in the eruption of Vesuvius). He has just been describing the Dead Sea and its marvels, and he continues thus:

> On its west side, just far enough from its shore to avoid its baneful influences, live the Essenes. They form a solitary community, and they inspire our admiration more than any other community in the whole world. They live without women (for they have renounced all sexual life), they live without money, and without any company save that of the palm trees. From day to day their numbers are maintained by the stream of people who seek them out and join them from far and wide. These people are driven to adopt the Essenes' way of life through weariness of ordinary life and by reason of the changes of fortune. Thus, through thousands of generations —incredible to relate—this community in which no one is ever born continues without dying; other people's weariness of life is the secret of their abiding fertility! Below their headquarters was the town of Engedi, whose fertility and palm-groves formerly made it second only to Jerusalem; but now, like Jerusalem itself, it lies a heap of ashes. Next comes Masada, a fortress on a rock, itself also not far from the Dead Sea. And there is the frontier of Judæa.

Whoever the people may be whom Pliny is describing, his description, which is probably based on earlier sources, contains a large element of rhetorical exaggeration. For example, the Essenes had certainly not lived in that area for "thousands of generations"; ten generations would probably be a considerable exaggeration, even if we reckoned four generations to a century. Therefore perhaps we should not conclude too hastily that Pliny cannot be referring to the Qumran community, even if we can immediately spot some features of his account which cannot be reconciled with the evidence we have collected thus far about that community. As was mentioned earlier, Father de Vaux concluded, shortly after the excavations at Khirbet Qumran were begun, that here were the headquarters below which (as Pliny said) lay the town of Engedi. And yet Khirbet Qumran itself provided evidence that the community which had its centre there lived neither without women nor without money, so that Pliny's statements on both these points would have to be taken with a grain of salt if Father de Vaux's identification were accepted.

Of the two Jewish writers who mention the Essenes, Philo of Alexandria was the earlier: he was born about 20 B.C. and died about A.D. 50. He has left us two accounts of the Essenes. One is a fairly long account, in his treatise *Every Good Man is Free* (which is commonly regarded as one of his more youthful productions); the other is shorter, and formed part of his *Hypothetics*, an apologetic work.

In his longer account Philo estimates the numbers of the Essenes at about four thousand, and describes them as living in villages, working hard at agriculture and similar occupations, devoting much time (especially on the sabbath, when they congregated in their synagogues) to the communal study of moral and religious questions, including the interpretation of the sacred scriptures. They paid scrupulous attention to ceremonial purity, he tells us, and held all their property—money, food and clothes—in common. They abstained from animal sacrifice, from the swearing of oaths, from military service and commercial activity. They kept no slaves, made provision for those of their number who were unable to work through sickness and old age, and in general cultivated all the virtues. They were, indeed, illustrious examples of his thesis that the truly good are the truly free.

In his shorter account Philo again makes mention of several of these features, and adds that they admit none but adults to membership in their community, and that they practise celibacy, on the ground that wives and families distract men's attention from the pursuit of goodness and truth.

Josephus, who was born about A.D. 37 and lived on to the end of the century, has also given us two accounts of the Essenes. His longer and earlier account comes in the second book of his *History of the Jewish War*, which was written only a few years after A.D. 70. A shorter account appears in the eighteenth book of his *Jewish Antiquities*, written some twenty years later.

Josephus gives us more detailed information than Philo does, and his information is based—in part, at least—on first-hand evidence. He claims, indeed, to have made trial of the Essenes in his youth, as of the other Jewish sects, in order that, when he had made some acquaintance with them all, he might choose the best. Unfortunately, we can never read anything that Josephus tells us about himself without a certain measure of reserve; and as his "close familiarity" with the Essenes was wedged in along with other experiences between his sixteenth and nineteenth years it does not appear to have been very extended.

Besides, while Philo for his part admittedly uses the Essenes to point a moral, Josephus in turn emphasizes those features in this as in other Jewish sects which he judged would make the greatest impression on his Gentile readers; for one thing, he persists in describing the Jewish religious sects as schools of philosophy after the Greek fashion.

For the most part, however, Josephus's description of the Essenes strikes us as being factual and reliable.

According to him the Essenes were scattered through all the cities of Palestine. Some of them lived in Jerusalem. They practised common hospitality; an Essene from a distance would be treated as a brother by any other Essene to whose house he came. But much of Josephus's description implies a community life such as could not be followed by permanent city-dwellers, and a reasonable inference is that the fully initiated Essenes were organized in separate communities while they had attached to them associate members who lived in cities.

In his shorter account of the sect he says:

> The doctrine of the Essenes is that all things are left in the hand of God. They teach the immortality of the soul, and think it their

duty to strive for the fruits of righteousness. When they send their votive offerings to the temple, they do not bring sacrifices, because they have distinctive purificatory rites of their own; for this reason they are excluded from the common precinct of the temple and offer their sacrifices by themselves. They excel all other men in their manner of life, and they devote themselves wholly to agriculture. A special meed of admiration should be accorded to their righteousness, in which they surpass all others who pursue the good life, without precedent among either Greeks or barbarians. Nor is this a temporary devotion; it has persisted among them for long as a settled policy. They have all things in common, so that a rich man enjoys no more of his wealth than a man who is penniless. There are more than four thousand men who follow this way of life, and they neither marry wives nor keep slaves, for they think that the possession of slaves tends to injustice, while marriage is an occasion of strife. But they live by themselves and serve one another. They appoint fit men to receive their revenues and the produce of the earth, and priests to supervise the preparation of their bread and other food. They all follow the same course of life without deviation.

While Josephus confirms, in general, the statements of Philo and Pliny that the Essenes were celibates, he mentions one order of Essenes, "which, while at one with the rest in its mode of life, customs and regulations, differs from them in its views on marriage." Members of this particular order marry wives and bring up families, he says, because they reckon that otherwise the race would die out (a naïve explanation, since, on his showing, the major Essene groups appear to have propagated their species quite successfully by adopting and bringing up other people's children). These wives evidently shared the community life and ritual washings.

Anyone who sought admission to the Essene brotherhood, Josephus tells us, had to undergo three years' probation. During the first year he wore the white habit and girdle which were characteristic of the sect, and carried the small trowel which every Essene used to dig a latrine-pit in accordance with the instruction of Deut. 23: 12–14. At the end of the first year the novice was admitted to the ritual purification in water, but two more years had to elapse before he was considered ready for admission to the communal meal. And when this final stage of full initiation was reached, says Josephus, "before he is allowed to touch the communal food, he is made to swear tremendous oaths: first, that he will practise piety towards God; then, that he will observe justice towards men; that he will do wrong to none whether on his own initiative or by another's orders; that he will always hate evildoers and help the just; that he will keep faith with all men and especially with those in authority (since no man achieves dominion save by the will of God); that, if he himself should be a ruler, he will not abuse his authority or outshine his subjects in dress or by any superior decoration; that he will always love truth and expose liars; that he will keep his hands free from theft and his soul pure from impious gain; that he will conceal nothing from his fellow-Essenes and reveal none of their secrets to others, even though he be tortured to death. He swears, moreover, to transmit their rules exactly as he received them, to abstain from banditry, and likewise to preserve the books of the sect and the names of the angels. By such oaths they bind securely those who join them."

As might be expected in a fellowship guarded by such oaths, the discipline was strict; yet it was notoriously and inflexibly just. The effect of the initiatory oaths on the conscience of those who were bound by them was such that an excommunicated Essene inevitably starved to death (unless his excommunication was rescinded in time), because all food prepared otherwise than according to their rule was ceremonially unclean and he could not bring himself to eat it. Josephus tells how many members of the sect endured all kinds of tortures at the hand of the Romans, who tried by such means to force them to eat forbidden food or otherwise break their oath, but all to no effect.

An Essene's day began before sunrise, when he rose to recite morning prayers along with his fellows, "as though they were entreating the sun to rise." Before these prayers were offered no word was spoken. Then (except on the sabbath, which was very strictly observed) the brethren betook themselves to the various tasks which were assigned to them by the overseers, and worked at them until noon was approaching. Then they assembled in the community centre, bathed, and entered the refectory in their linen habits. This midday meal was a solemn occasion at which none but full members were present. It was introduced and concluded by grace, said by a priest, and the company praised God together before and after the meal, which consisted of simple fare. They ate in moderation, and their behaviour during the meal, as at all other times, was marked by quietness and sobriety. They did not all speak at once, but spoke in turn, observing the rules of seniority. For there were four classes of members, arranged in order of seniority.

After the meal they laid aside their linen habits, resumed their working clothes, and continued at their prescribed tasks until evening. Then they assembled for another meal, but at this meal strangers and visitors might be present.

One curious feature which Josephus relates for the edification of his readers is that the Essenes regarded oil as defiling and would not anoint themselves, even after bathing, for they believed a rough skin to be more pleasing to heaven. They avoided oaths, apart from those which they swore at their initiation. They were great students of the sacred books and writings of the ancients, and had a reputation both for interpreting the prophets and for making predictions themselves, which were regularly verified by the event. They also paid much attention to the medicinal properties of various roots, plants and "stones" (probably bituminous products of the Dead Sea).

Another writer who gives us an account of the Essenes on the general lines of Josephus's account is the Roman Christian Hippolytus, whose treatise on *The Refutation of All Heresies* dates from the early years of the third century. Hippolytus appears to have had access to a reliable and independent source of information, which enabled him to correct Josephus's account in certain points, and to supplement it in others. Hippolytus omits the suggestion of sun-worship in their morning prayers; according to him, "they continue in prayer from early dawn, and do not speak a word until they have sung a hymn of praise to God." Hippolytus's omission of anything that looks like sun-worship would not be due to a desire to make the Essenes more orthodox than they really were; perhaps Josephus had in mind a sect called the Sampsaeans, which probably had some affinities with the Essenes, and acquired their name (derived from the Semitic word for "sun") from acts of homage paid to the sun as a manifestation of divinity. The term Essenes, in fact, was used at times to cover a wide range of Jewish sectarian groups that drew aside from the main stream of life; Hippolytus himself includes within them some people whose characteristics, we should think, attached them to the Zealots and marked them off from the Essenes.

Hippolytus gives us a number of instances which illustrate the strictness with which the Essenes observed the sabbath and other laws. Some, he says, would not handle a coin which bore the likeness of the emperor or any other man, for the very act of looking at such a thing was regarded by them as one of the forms of idolatry forbidden in the Second Commandment.

But his most important deviation from Josephus's account is his statement that the Essenes believed in the resurrection of the body, as well as in the immortality of the soul. The soul, he says, is in their view imperishable, and rests after death in an airy and well-lighted place, until the day of judgment arrives and it is rejoined by the resurrected body. But Josephus tells us that the Essenes regarded the body as the temporary and perishable prison-house of the immortal soul, from which at death the latter breaks free and soars on high, rejoicing at its liberation from a long bondage. Both bear witness to the Essene belief in the natural immortality of the soul, which was not a characteristic doctrine of Judaism, but Josephus, not content with recording this Greek element in Essene belief, appears to have made a further concession to Greek taste by implying that the Essenes did not expect a bodily resurrection.

According to Philo, the Essenes were founded by Moses. No doubt, like the men who transmitted the main body of Jewish religious tradition, they represented their regulations and interpretations of the law as going back to Moses and bearing his authority. And when Josephus tells us that they honoured the name of their law-giver next after the name of God, and punished any blasphemous or unseemly use of his name with death, he is probably referring to Moses (although it has been suggested more recently that the law-giver in question was the Teacher of Righteousness). But their existence as a community cannot be traced back earlier than the closing years of the second century B.C. The first Essene known to history is a man called Judah, who lived in the reign of the Hasmonean king Aristobulus I (104–103 B.C.) and was renowned for his ability to predict the future.

The derivation of the name "Essene" has long been, and still is, a matter of debate; but most probably it comes from an Aramaic word meaning "pious" or "holy," corresponding in sense to the Hebrew *hasid*. In fact the Essenes probably represent one line of development of the movement of the *hasidim*, who played a leading part (as we have seen) in resisting Antiochus Epiphanes. Another line of development may be recognized in the rise and growth of the party of the Pharisees from the latter decades of the second century B.C. onwards. But we have already suggested that the movement which found a leader in the Teacher of Righteousness also arose from the ranks of the *hasidim*.

What, then, was the relation between the Essenes and the Qumran community? Are we to make a straightforward identification of the two movements, or is there some other, fairly close, connexion between the two which falls short of outright identity?

Almost from the early days of the discoveries in Cave 1 at Qumran, an identification of the community with the Essenes has been suggested. Professor Sukenik was one of the first to do so. Father de Vaux identified Khirbet Qumran with the Essene headquarters mentioned by Pliny. Professor Dupont-Sommer has popularized the idea in two books, translated into English under the titles *The Dead Sea Scrolls* (1952) and *The Jewish Sect of Qumran and the Essenes* (1954). And several other writers have favoured the view that the Qumran community was an Essene group.

What are the arguments in favour of the identification?

We have noted the geographical argument in favour of identifying Khirbet Qumran with the Essene headquarters below which, according to Pliny, the town of Engedi lay. This argument depends on our taking "below" to mean not lower in relation to sea-level, but farther south, as on a map of normal orientation.

Then there is a chronological argument: the Essenes are known to have flourished during the time when the Qumran community was in being—they make their appearance in history about the same time as the beginning of the Qumran movement, towards the end of the second century B.C., and were still flourishing in the second half of the first century A.D.

More important is the argument based on the similarity between the beliefs and practices of the Essenes, as contemporary writers describe them, and those of the Qumran community, as attested in their own literature.

There are striking similarities (which do not, however, amount to complete identity) between the two in respect of the long period of probation, the solemn oaths sworn on initiation, the strict discipline, the baptismal washings, the common meal, the hierarchical organization with exact observance of the rules of precedence, the place of honour and responsibility given to priests, the community of goods, the rigorous interpretation of the sabbath law and the pursuit of an unusually high and exacting standard of righteousness. Since the *Rule of the Community* makes it clear that a common penalty at Qumran was the reduction of rations, we can easily understand how a member whose offence was so serious as to warrant complete withdrawal of rations for a sufficiently long time could be in danger of death by starvation, as Josephus tells us. Sometimes the similarity between the two disciplinary codes extends to matters which we should regard as trivial; thus Josephus's statement that the Essenes avoided spitting "into the midst" or to the right is paralleled by the regulation in the *Rule of the Community* that a man who "spits into the midst of the session of the many" shall be punished—by suspension from a share in the communal meal?—for thirty days.

From Josephus's statement that "if ten are in session together, no one of them will speak if the other nine are against it" we might reasonably infer that ten was a normal grouping of their membership, and this reminds us that at Qumran ten might engage in the regular communal activities provided that the ten included a priest. But since ten was a recognized number for communal activity among the Jews in general (to this day it is the quorum necessary for a synagogue congregation among orthodox Jews), no weight can be put on this coincidence.

Josephus's testimony to the Essenes' intensive study of the ancient scriptures, particularly the prophetic writings, may find ample illustration in the Qumran texts. On the other hand, the instances he gives of the Essenes' gift of prophecy appear trivial in comparison with the forecasts of coming events, based on the interpretation of Old Testament prophecy, which we find in the Qumran texts. His reference to the Essene interest in angels is in keeping with the attention which was paid at Qumran to late Jewish works in which angels figure prominently.

Hippolytus tells us that the Essenes expected a universal conflagration at the time of the last judgment; this belief finds expression in the Qumran *Hymns of Thanksgiving*, in terms which suggest Zoroastrian influence:

The foundations of the mountains are burned up;
The roots of flint become torrents of pitch:
It devours even to the great abyss;
The torrents of Belial break forth into Abaddon.

But, in spite of all the similarities and parallels that can be adduced, we cannot feel too happy about an outright identification of the Qumran community with the Essenes. Where prominent features of the one body are not related at all in the sources of our information about the other, we cannot reach indisputable conclusions. Again, both bodies no doubt modified their beliefs and practices to some extent in the course of the years, so that we should not lay too much emphasis, perhaps, on divergencies between the Essenes and Qumran with regard to the frequency and significance of baptismal lustration, the years during which a man's probation lasted, sacrificial doctrine and procedure, the attitude towards the government (Jewish or Gentile) and the use of force. Yet there are so many hints in ancient writings of a bewildering variety of messianic and baptist groups with their headquarters in the Jordan valley and Dead Sea region that we should be cautious before we make a complete identification of two of these groups concerning which we are now better informed than we are about the others.

A tentative identification may, however, be made of our friends at Qumran with the marrying Essenes of whom Josephus has something to tell us. It seems quite clear that the Qumran community did not abjure marriage, although they did maintain a very strict interpretation of the Jewish marriage law (forbidding polygamy and unions between uncle and niece). But if this tentative identification is confirmed by further evidence, it must be recognized that Josephus's marrying Essenes were very exceptional Essenes, for not only Pliny and Philo but Josephus himself record celibacy as one of the characteristic features of the Essenes in general. It is very probable that Josephus uses the name "Essenes" in a narrower and in a wider sense, and that only in its wider sense can the Qumran community be included under this designation.

The Essenes are mentioned only in Greek and Latin documents. It may be asked whether the Qumran community can be identified with any group mentioned in Jewish rabbinical literature, which is written in Hebrew and Aramaic. Here too we are unable thus far to say anything certain. We may think of those people known to rabbinical tradition as the "morning bathers" because they indulged in a ritual washing at dawn before they took the name of God upon their lips—thus exceeding the righteousness of the Pharisees, with whom they entered into controversy. But in view of the variety of baptist sects in the Judaism of those days, a verdict of "Not Proven" is all that our present knowledge warrants.

CHAPTER XI

QUMRAN AND CHRISTIANITY

WHAT happened to the Qumran community after the abandonment of their headquarters in A.D. 68? Neither the archaeological evidence on the site nor the contents of their library can in the nature of the case give us a direct answer to this question. But it need not remain completely unanswered.

It may be that the torments which Josephus describes as inflicted by Romans on members of the Essene sect, to force them to violate their solemn oaths, were endured by some of the fugitives from Qumran, as well as by members of similar groups. But some at least would escape with their lives. Their beliefs and expectations would inevitably undergo considerable modification by reason of the events of A.D. 70, but they would not be changed beyond recognition. And there is some evidence that certain beliefs and practices akin to those maintained at Qumran reappeared in other communities, possibly under the influence of men of Qumran who escaped the destruction.

Professor Oscar Cullmann, for example, has pointed out that we may have to reconsider the whole question of the origin of the Mandaeans, a fascinating Mesopotamian sect of gnostic belief and baptist practice,[1] in the light of the new evidence from Qumran. This is certainly a matter for re-examination. But there is another sect whose beliefs and practices call for fresh study in the light of the new discoveries. This is the Ebionite sect, consisting of Jewish Christians who deviated considerably not only from the main stream of Catholic Christianity but also from the Christianity enshrined in the New Testament, even in its earliest and most Jewish stages.[2] There is now some reason to suppose that several of these Ebionite deviations, in doctrine and procedure, were introduced under the influence of men from Qumran in the years following A.D. 70.

[1] Cf. *The Growing Day*, p. 182.

[2] Cf. *The Growing Day*, pp. 172 ff. The fact that the Qumran covenanters, like these Jewish Christians, called themselves *'ebyonim* (i.e. the "poor") is one of Dr. Teicher's arguments for identifying the two groups.

We are told that, before the siege of Jerusalem began, the disciples of Jesus in that city, believing in its impending doom, fled to Pella, east of the Jordan. It would not really be surprising if they were joined there by others who fled from the Roman vengeance. That these others may have included refugees from Qumran is rendered the more probable by striking affinities in thought and practice which have been detected by a comparison of parts of the later Ebionite literature with the literature of Qumran. It would be going too far to say that Ebionitism represents an amalgamation of primitive Jewish Christianity and the system of Qumran, for Ebionitism remained fundamentally Christian; but the particular emphasis and direction which made Ebionite Christianity so distinctive can be explained rather convincingly in terms of its incorporation of remnants from Qumran. Two European scholars who have paid special attention to this fascinating possibility are Professor Cullmann[1] and Professor H. J. Schoeps,[2] both of whom had established their reputations as authorities in the Ebionite field before the Dead Sea Scrolls came to light.

But, no matter how interesting this question is, there is another more interesting by far. Did the Qumran community have any influence on Christianity, or at least some contact with it, *before* the dispersal of A.D. 68? If (as seems probable) the Qumran community was established before the birth of Christ, was Christianity in any way indebted to it? And, more generally, do the Qumran discoveries give us fresh help in understanding the New Testament?

When the discovery of the scrolls was first announced, it was believed by many that their chief importance would lie in the new light which they could throw on the history of the Old Testament text. And, as has been indicated in an earlier chapter, the light which they throw on this field of study is of high value. But with the emergence and examination of so many more docu-

[1] A particularly powerful argument for the incorporation of the remnants of the Qumran movement in this stream of Jewish Christianity is given by Professor Cullmann in his essay "Die neuentdeckten Qumran-Texte und das Judenchristentum der Pseudoklementinen," contributed to the recent volume of *Neutestamentliche Studien* presented to Rudolf Bultmann (1954), pp. 35 ff. Cf. also his article on "The Significance of the Qumran Texts for Research into the Beginnings of Christianity" in the *Journal of Biblical Literature* 74 (1955), pp. 213 ff.

[2] Cf. his *Urgemeinde, Judenchristentum, Gnosis* (1956), pp. 69 ff.

ments from the neighbourhood, and the excavation of Khirbet Qumran, the emphasis has changed more and more from the Old Testament to the New Testament side. Few greater misstatements of fact have been made in all the literature which the Qumran discoveries have called forth than one which Mr. Edmund Wilson makes in *The Scrolls from the Dead Sea* (p. 131): "New Testament scholars, it seems, have almost without exception boycotted the whole subject of the scrolls." I read these words with the more surprise as I had, a few weeks before, attended the 1955 meeting of the international *Studiorum Novi Testamenti Societas*, at which no subject aroused more animated discussion than the implications of Qumran for New Testament study. A glance at the list of contents of two recently founded journals, *New Testament Studies* (Cambridge) and *Novum Testamentum* (Leiden), suffices to show the baselessness of Mr. Wilson's remark. One does not demand from a non-specialist the kind of knowledge which only an expert could reasonably be expected to possess; but one does look for a higher degree of factual accuracy than this.

Opinions differ widely on the bearing which the Qumran discoveries may have on the rise and early progress of Christianity. And the reason of this wide difference of opinion is quite simple. It is that, among the documents published to date, no unambiguous evidence has come to light which affords a direct contact with Christian origins. Very much depends on varying individual interpretations by those who have studied the texts. So, on the one hand, Father Kevan Smyth, an Irish Jesuit scholar, says that to compare the scrolls with the New Testament without taking into account the wealth of relevant information from the later Old Testament, apocryphal, pseudepigraphic and rabbinical literature, "is like comparing a fish and a man because both are wet after coming out of the sea." Against those who have seen in Qumran the soil from which Christianity sprang, he says: "Rather, it was from soil such as this that sprang the thorns which tried to choke the seed of the Gospel."[1]

On the other hand, we have Dr. J. L. Teicher maintaining that the Teacher of Righteousness was none other than Jesus, while the Qumran community consisted of Jewish Christians of the kind commonly known as Ebionites. Dr. Teicher's arguments, which have been published in several issues of the *Journal of*

[1] *The Irish Digest*, June, 1956, pp. 31–34 (condensed from *Studies*).

Jewish Studies, have not convinced other scholars, although he has commented on the paradoxical situation that he, a Jewish scholar, finds himself defending the originality of Jesus against some Christian scholars who have found in the Teacher of Righteousness one who anticipated the teaching, passion and messianic claims of Jesus and have seen in the Qumran community an adumbration of the primitive Christian Church.

Among the scholars who have taken this latter line are Professor Dupont-Sommer and Mr. J. M. Allegro. We have mentioned some of their arguments in the chapter on "The Teacher of Righteousness." Professor Dupont-Sommer concluded that "the Galilæan Teacher, as he is presented to us in the New Testament writings, appears in many respects as an astonishing reincarnation of the Teacher of Righteousness."[1] Mr. Allegro says that the expectations of the early Church with regard to the Second Coming of Christ "are extraordinarily like those of the sect about their own Teacher, persecuted and crucified, and expected to rise again as priestly Messiah." He adds: "It now seems probable that the Church took over the sect's way of life, their discipline, much of their doctrine, and certainly a good deal of their phraseology, in which it is now seen that the New Testament abounds."[2]

It is such views as these that were popularized by Mr. Wilson in his book mentioned above; on the strength of them he hazards the suggestion that Khirbet Qumran "is perhaps, more than Bethlehem or Nazareth, the cradle of Christianity" (p. 129). And it was on the strength of such views, doubtless, that a distinguished archaeologist wrote in the course of an article on Khirbet Qumran in the *Illustrated London News* of September 3, 1955: "John the Baptist was almost certainly an Essene, and must have studied and worked in this building; he undoubtedly derived the idea of ritual immersion, or baptism, from them. Many authorities consider that Christ Himself also studied with them for some time. If that be so, then we have in this little building something unique indeed, for alone of all the ancient remains in Jordan, this has remained unchanged—indeed, unseen and unknown, to this day. These, then, are the very walls He looked upon, the corridors and rooms through which He wandered and

[1] *Aperçus préliminaires sur les Manuscrits de la Mer Morte* (1950), p. 121. Cf. the English translation, *The Dead Sea Scrolls* (1952), p. 99.

[2] *The Radio Times*, January 13, 1956, p. 9. See his letter to *The Times*, March 20, 1956.

in which He sat . . ." These are no more than theories, although the theory of John the Baptist's association with Qumran is less improbable than that of our Lord's residence there. But when a well-known archaeological authority states these theories in such unqualified terms, the ordinary reader may reasonably suppose that there is some archaeological evidence for them, and thus far there is none.

In so far as theories of this kind are based on the supposition that the Teacher of Righteousness claimed to be a Messiah, or that his followers believed him to be one, they have been dealt with already in this book; and it may suffice to repeat here that there is no evidence that the Teacher ever made such claims for himself, or that his followers ever thought of him as a messianic figure. We do not know the circumstances in which he died—or "was gathered in," to use the Qumran phraseology. Nor is it suggested in the published texts that his followers attached any saving significance to his death. If they believed that he would be raised again in advance of the more general resurrection which Dan. 12:2 taught them to expect, then they thought that his resurrection ministry would be a preparation for the imminent arrival of the Messiahs of Aaron and Israel. Their expectation corresponded to the expectation which many of their fellow-Jews cherished with regard to the prophet Elijah. Elijah, it was widely believed (on the basis of Mal. 4: 5 f.), would one day return to earth from that realm to which he had been snatched away in a whirlwind so many centuries before; and his return would be a signal of the near approach of "the great and terrible day of the LORD," for which his new ministry would prepare the people. Jesus taught His disciples to recognize the fulfilment of this expectation in the ministry of John the Baptist, His own precursor. But the Qumran sect apparently linked it with the expected resurrection of their Teacher, although there is nothing to suggest that they thought of the Teacher, even in resurrection, as a reincarnation of Elijah.[1] However that may be, the Teacher was in their eyes a preparer of the way for the messianic age, and not a messianic personage himself.

Professor Cullmann thus goes too far when he says that if Jesus knew about the Teacher of Righteousness, He probably included

[1] Neither did they identify him with the other eschatological prophet, the second Moses who was expected in fulfilment of Deut. 18: 15. See pp. 77–80.

him in the sweeping condemnation of John 10: 8: "All who came before me are thieves and robbers." Had the Teacher made messianic claims for himself, he would no doubt have been included in this condemnation; but Jesus certainly did not wish to characterize the prophets and righteous men of earlier days as "thieves and robbers." In fact, we may agree that the Teacher was indeed a preparer of the way for the Messiah, although not in a sense which either he or his disciples would have recognized at the time.

Those who deny so emphatically the messianic character of the Teacher of Righteousness are not necessarily moved by prejudice or an excessive preference for their accepted traditions; their concern is rather that at this stage in the inquiry students should not run too far in advance of the documentary evidence. But on the other hand those scholars who, like Professor Dupont-Sommer, draw inferences which their colleagues believe to be unwarranted should not have unworthy motives ascribed to them, as though (for example) they were over-anxious to deny the originality of Jesus and the element of divine revelation in Christianity. Scholars may disagree violently with one another's interpretations, and engage vigorously in debate; far more progress will be achieved in this way than by a mute agreement to differ. But when suspicion is thrown upon their intellectual integrity or the purity of their motives, a barrier is placed in the way of that fertile intercourse of minds to which the advancement of knowledge owes so much.

The wilderness of Judæa, in which the covenanters of Qumran established their place of retreat, figures in the Gospel narrative now and then. It was there (according to Matt. 3: 1) that John the Baptist began his public preaching; it was there that Jesus spent the forty days of temptation (Matt. 4: 1); it was there, too, that Jesus spent a few quiet days with His disciples before His last visit to Jerusalem (John 11: 54). But the wilderness of Judæa was a much wider area than the immediate vicinity of Qumran, and it was possible to spend quite a long time in the wilderness without ever coming into touch with the Qumran community.

Still, some possibilities are more probable than others. And little can be urged, in terms of probability, against the possibility that John the Baptist at one stage of his career had some contact with the Qumran covenanters or with some other people very like them. At the end of Luke's account of the birth and infancy of John, he says that "the child grew and became strong in spirit, and he was in the wilderness till the day of his manifestation to Israel" (Luke 1: 80). The implication of these words is that, for a number of years preceding the start of his baptismal ministry, John resided in the wilderness of Judæa. Now, if a congenial retreat was found there by a youth who was born in a city of Judæa and was later to be active in the Jordan valley, it would not have been far from the neighbourhood of Qumran. And one who was of priestly birth, as John was, might have found something specially appealing in a movement which attached such importance to the preservation of a pure priesthood.

A further contact between John and Qumran might be looked for in their baptismal teaching and practice. But it is a curious fact that Josephus's account of John's baptismal teaching accords more closely with the Qumran doctrine than does the New Testament account. When we read in the *Rule of the Community* that the man who is impure and rebellious in heart cannot hope to be cleansed by ritual washing in water, we are reminded of Josephus's statement that John "taught that baptism would be regarded as acceptable by God provided that they underwent it not to procure pardon for certain sins but with a view to the purification of the body when once the soul had been purified by righteousness." Josephus's statement differs, in emphasis at least, from the New Testament description of John's baptism as "a baptism of repentance for the remission of sins." It may well be that Josephus, who was not born until some eight years after John's death, interpreted his baptismal activity in terms of a baptismal doctrine with which he himself was more familiar—the doctrine of the Essenes. But if that is so, it would follow that John's baptismal doctrine represented a deviation—perhaps a deliberate one—from that of the Qumran covenanters and other Essenes.

John was an ascetic; he came, we are told, "eating no bread and drinking no wine" (Luke 7: 33). The Qumran covenanters were ascetics too, but not to that extent. Their food was simple, to be sure, and they ate in moderation, but they did not restrict themselves to locusts and wild honey, as John did. John proclaimed the urgent necessity of repentance, because "The Coming One" was about to execute a purifying judgment with wind and fire. The Qumran covenanters also thought in terms of an imminent judgment, but they were not the only people who did so, and they did not issue a public call to national repentance, as John did.

John may have had some contact with the Qumran community; he may even have belonged to it for a time. There is no real evidence of this at present, but if some evidence to this effect came to light, it would be welcomed by a number of students as confirmation of something which they had already surmised. One South African scholar,[1] indeed, finds hints in the first two chapters of St. Luke's Gospel that the statement already quoted ("the child grew and became strong in spirit, and he was in the wilderness until the day of his manifestation to Israel") represents a compression of a fuller account. According to this fuller account, he thinks, John's parents (who were both well on in years when he was born) died while he was still quite young, and he was adopted and brought up by the Essenes of Qumran. This may have been so. But in the present state of our certain knowledge, such a reconstruction belongs more to the realm of historical fiction than to that of real history.

But even if John did owe some debt to the Qumran community, or to any other Essene group, the ministry by which John made his mark cannot be brought within an Essene framework. He describes himself as a voice crying to Israel:

> In the wilderness prepare ye the way of the LORD;
> Make straight in the desert a highway for our God.

These words of Isa. 40: 3 had already been invoked by the Qumran covenanters as divine authority for their withdrawal to the wilderness. But John used them in a new sense. The divine intervention foretold by the prophet, of which the return of the exiles in the time of Cyrus was but a preliminary earnest, was about to be fulfilled. And it was a new impulse which sent John forth "to make ready for the Lord a people prepared" (Luke 1: 17). His recorded ministry is distinctively and essentially a prophetic ministry. And when "the word of God came to John the son of Zechariah in the wilderness" (Luke 3: 2), as it

[1] A. S. Geyser, "The Youth of John the Baptist," *Novum Testamentum* 1 (1956), pp. 70 ff. Cf. W. H. Brownlee, "John the Baptist in the New Light of Ancient Scrolls," *Interpretation* 9 (1955), pp. 71 ff.

had come to many a prophet before, he learned and proclaimed the necessity of something more than the teaching or action of Qumran. If he had previously been associated with that community or a similar one, it was now time to break with them and follow a new path, marked out for him by God. The multitudes that flocked to the Jordan valley to hear him did so because they recognized in his preaching a note of authority the like of which had not been heard in Israel for many a long day; "all held that John was a real prophet" (Mark 11: 32). It is not as a disciple of the Teacher of Righteousness, but as a new teacher of righteousness who had his own following of disciples, that we know the historical John the Baptist.

If the present state of our knowledge does not permit us to speak more positively about the possible contact between John the Baptist and Qumran, what can be said about Jesus Himself in this regard? John at least was an ascetic; but Jesus, on His own testimony, was not. To those who found fault with John's ministry and His own alike, He said: "John the Baptist has come eating no bread and drinking no wine; and you say, 'He has a demon.' The Son of man has come eating and drinking; and you say, 'Behold, a glutton and a drunkard, a friend of tax collectors and sinners!'" There is no flavour of Qumran about His way of life. Again, John at least is known to have lived in the wilderness before he began his public ministry; so far as we know, Jesus lived in Galilee continuously from His childhood to His baptism, apart from an occasional festival visit to Jerusalem. It was from Nazareth that He came to be baptized by John, and only after that did He retire to the wilderness of Judæa. The forty days that He spent there fasting would not afford much opportunity of initiation into the wisdom of Qumran, if indeed He spent them anywhere in that vicinity. (The traditional site of the temptation is some three miles north-west of Jericho, but that is of no significance.) The temptations which He experienced in the wilderness are usually (and no doubt rightly) explained as temptations to achieve His messianic destiny by other paths than that of the Suffering Servant, marked out for Him at His baptism; and among those other paths which He repudiated the way of Qumran, in certain of its aspects, must be included.

It is easy to go through the recorded teaching of Jesus and list parallels—some of them quite impressive—with what we find in the Qumran texts. This sort of thing has been done already in relation to the Gospels and rabbinic literature. It has long been known that some kind of parallel can be found in the Talmud to practically every element in the ethical teaching of Jesus. It is idle to feel alarm at this, as though the originality of Jesus and the divine authority of Christianity were imperilled by such a recognition. For He accepted the same Biblical revelation as did the Qumran covenanters and the rabbis in the main stream of Jewish tradition, and it would be surprising if no affinity at all were found between their interpretations of that revelation, on which their teachings were based.

It has often been pointed out, for example, that in His interpretation of the Old Testament marriage law our Lord approximated to the Pharisaic school of Shammai rather than to that of Hillel—surprisingly, some have felt, because in general the Pharisaism which He condemned was that of the school of Shammai. Even so, there was an important difference between His attitude and that of both Pharisaic schools. For Shammai and Hillel's difference in this regard arose from their divergent interpretations of the legal prescription of Deut. 24: 1–4, where divorce is permitted for "some unseemly thing" in the wife. The two schools disagreed on the definition of "some unseemly thing." But our Lord dismissed this legal prescription as a temporary concession made because of men's hardness of heart, and insisted that the marriage law should be interpreted in the light of the original purpose of the institution: "From the beginning of creation, 'God made them male and female.' . . . What therefore God has joined together, let not man put asunder" (Mark 10: 6–9). To these words we find a closer verbal similarity in one of the Qumran texts than we find in any of our rabbinical sources. In a passage in the Zadokite *Admonition* certain people are condemned "for taking two wives in their lifetime, although the basic principle of creation is 'He created them male and female,' and those that went into the ark 'went into the ark two by two.'" Here the appeal to the Creator's institution of marriage is found, as in the teaching of Jesus. But the resemblance may be mainly verbal. It is polygamy rather than divorce that the *Admonition* condemns (divorce under certain conditions is permitted in the Zadokite *Laws*); and what the author of the *Admonition* is really attacking is the teaching of those rabbis who permitted polygamy. To him polygamy is a form of fornication ,and so is another practice which was condoned by the same rabbis—marriage between uncles and nieces.

When we come to the interpretation of the sabbath law (which first led to an open cleavage between Jesus and the rabbis of His day), we do not find even a verbal similarity between the Gospels and the Qumran texts. In the Gospels it is taken for granted that even the strictest rabbis would allow a domestic animal to be rescued if it fell into a pit or cistern on the sabbath day. But the sabbath regulations in the Zadokite *Laws* are more stringent. A human being may be rescued under such conditions, but not an animal. "Let no one assist a beast in birth on the sabbath day. Even if she drops her new-born young into a cistern or pit, let him not lift it up on the sabbath." About twenty-five sabbath regulations are listed among the Zadokite *Laws*, and they are totally incompatible with the attitude expressed in Jesus' words: "The sabbath was made for man, not man for the sabbath" (Mark 2: 27). For Jesus' interpretation of the sabbath law, as of the law of marriage, was based on the purpose for which the sabbath was originally instituted.

One very interesting point of contact between the Qumran texts and the New Testament has been emphasized by a number of scholars recently, notably by Professor W. F. Albright in his Pelican book *The Archaeology of Palestine* and in a paper on "Recent Discoveries in Palestine and the Gospel of St. John" which he contributed to *The Background of the New Testament and its Eschatology* (a volume of essays published in 1956 in honour of Professor C. H. Dodd). This point of contact is found in a comparison of the distinctive vocabulary of the Fourth Gospel with that of some of the Qumran documents.[1] Such characteristic Johannine expressions as "the sons of light," "the light of life," "walking in darkness," "doing the truth," "the works of God," turn up in the writings of the Qumran community. Like the Qumran community, John sees the universe in terms of sharply contrasted light and darkness, good and evil, truth and falsehood. If Professor Albright's conclusion is valid, that John (and other New Testament writers as well) "draw from a common reservoir of terminology and ideas which were well known to

[1] See also Lucetta Mowry, "The Dead Sea Scrolls and the Gospel of John," *The Biblical Archaeologist* 17 (1954), pp. 78 ff. *Cf.* p. 140.

the Essenes and presumably familiar also to other Jewish sects of the period," scholars may be less inclined to trace these features to Hellenistic sources. Some may bethink themselves at this stage of the high probability that the Beloved Disciple was a follower of John the Baptist before he was called by Jesus. But the affinities in vocabulary should not make us overlook the new element in John's use of these terms. When he speaks of the true light, he is not thinking in abstractions; he is not primarily concerned with a body of teaching or a holy community; to him the true light is identical with Jesus Christ, the Word made flesh. And Professor Albright wisely emphasizes the "wide gulf between the doctrines of the Essenes and the essentials of Johannine teaching." He lists four essentials of the teaching of John (and of the Synoptic and Pauline teaching too); these relate to the function of the Messiah, the salvation of sinners, the ministry of healing, and the gospel of love.

The Qumran ritual washings were no doubt instituted in the light of God's promise in Ezek. 36: 25, that He would purify His people from their uncleanness by sprinkling clean water on them. The same promise also underlies the words of Jesus to Nicodemus in John 3: 5 about the necessity of a new birth "of water and the Spirit" for anyone who would enter the kingdom of God. But in the latter place this new birth is bound up with faith in Jesus and consequent union with Him and sharing of His eternal life. Jesus has filled the old words with a new content.

Such features of early Christian life as baptism and the breaking of bread, the rules of fellowship laid down in Matt. 18, the community of goods in the primitive Jerusalem church, the government of the group by apostles, elders and financial officers, have their analogues in the Qumran organization. But their significance within the Christian community is controlled by the person and work of Jesus. This Messiah was different from any kind of Messiah expected at Qumran or elsewhere in Israel in those days, and all the accompaniments of messianic expectation had their meaning transformed in the light of His messianic achievement.

The Qumran covenanters bound themselves by a new covenant, but it was not so new as they thought; it was a specially solemn and binding reaffirmation of the old covenant of Moses' day, by which the people of Israel pledged themselves to obey the law of God. What the people as a whole had failed to do, they would do as a righteous Israel within Israel, and do it so faithfully that their obedience would compensate for their brethren's disobedience. But the new age to which they looked forward was a revival of the best ideals of the old age. They looked forward to a new temple, a pure sacrificial worship, and the reinstatement of a worthy priesthood; but the temple would still be a building made with hands, the sacrificial worship would still involve the slaughter of bulls and goats, the priesthood would still be confined to the sons of Aaron. There is nothing here which presents an affinity to the Johannine narrative of Christ's changing of the water of Jewish purification into the wine of the new age. At Qumran the cadres of priests and Levites were carefully preserved in view of the day when they would resume their service in Jerusalem; there is nothing like this in primitive Christianity. In the early days of the Jerusalem church, we are told, "a great many of the priests were obedient to the faith" (Acts 6: 7); but there is not the slightest hint that they retained their priestly status and privileges within the Christian community.

Similarly, as we have seen, there can be no comparison between the Aaronic Messiah expected by the Qumran covenanters and the High Priest after the order of Melchizedek who is portrayed in the Epistle to the Hebrews.

But what about the Davidic Messiah—the Messiah of Israel—whom they also expected?

The Davidic Messiah, in Qumran expectation, would arise in the last days to deliver Israel, born from the travail of the righteous community. He would be the victorious captain of the sons of light in the last conflict with the sons of darkness, and in the new age following that victory he would enjoy a position as prince, second only to the priestly Messiah.

In its essentials this expectation of a Davidic Messiah was shared by many other Israelites (probably by the vast majority). And Jesus repudiated this kind of Messiahship as wholeheartedly as He could, from the days of the wilderness temptation right on to His death. He did not deny that He was the Messiah of David's line, but He made no such claim publicly, and forbade His disciples to make it on His behalf, because He knew that it would be misunderstood. Indeed, His refusal to accept the kingship which the people of Galilee tried to force upon Him caused considerable disillusionment among many who had followed Him up to that point. If He had envisaged His messianic task as the launching of a holy war, He would have found thousands of enthusiastic and devoted followers. But it is as certain as anything can be that He rejected the whole conception of such a warfare—whether in the immediate Zealot form or in the deferred Qumran form—in favour of the way of the Suffering Servant.

The Qumran covenanters set themselves to fulfil the rôle of the Servant, but they do not appear to have thought of any of their messianic figures as fulfilling it. Jesus, on the other hand, took the fulfilment of the Servant's rôle upon Himself as the very essence of His messianic mission. He combines in His one person the functions of Prophet, Priest and King; Servant of the Lord, Son of Man, and Teacher of Righteousness. In Him the hope of Israel greets its consummation, but in a way which exceeds all expectation. "To him," said one of His disciples (and all the others would have agreed), "all the prophets bear witness that every one who believes in him receives forgiveness of sins through his name" (Acts 10: 43). And if it is true that, after they were forced to abandon their community headquarters, some of the Qumran covenanters made common cause with the refugees from the Jerusalem church, they may have realized that the hopes which their community had cherished so long were fulfilled not in the way which they had expected but by the death and resurrection of Jesus of Nazareth.

Noble as the mission of the Qumran community was, to fill the rôle of the Servant of the Lord, that rôle could never be adequately filled by withdrawal from contact with sinners. The perfect Servant, when He came, was criticized because He welcomed sinners and accepted invitations to their homes. But the Pharisees, who criticized Him thus, would themselves have been criticized by the men of Qumran for their quite inadequate separation from sinners. Yet, if sinners are to be delivered from their sin and changed into new men and women, it must be by one whose friendship towards them is real, unaffected, and unlimited. He who was called the friend of sinners in His lifetime has been known as the friend of sinners ever since.

Ernest Renan described Christianity as "an Essenism which has largely succeeded."[1] Why did it succeed when Essenism disappeared? Partly, I should say, because it contained every-

[1] *Histoire du peuple d'Israël*, v (1893), p. 70.

thing that there was of abiding value in Essenism—and much besides. But, pre-eminently, Christianity owes not only its survival but its very being and character to Jesus. The community of Qumran owed much to the enigmatic figure of the Teacher of Righteousness and his original and inspiring interpretation of prophecy. But Jesus not only interpreted Old Testament prophecy; He carried His interpretation into effect and so became Himself the living fulfilment of Old Testament prophecy. Nor does this fulfilment come to a full stop with His death and resurrection: it goes on in His abiding ministry through His followers, so long as they carry out in His Spirit the charge laid upon the Servant long ago (Isa. 49: 6):

> I will give you as a light to the nations,
> That my salvation may reach to the end of the earth.

EPILOGUE

As this book goes to press, rumours are persistently circulating about further exciting discoveries of manuscripts from Qumran. One rumour tells of manuscripts of great importance which have been found in an eleventh cave in that area, including complete texts of Leviticus and the Psalter. Another speaks of a scroll containing the five books of Moses. A good deal of mystery appears to envelop some of these latest discoveries. Towards the end of May (1956) the press in this country and America reported Professor Albright as saying that two scrolls had been stolen by Bedouin from under the noses of their guardians; but his statement was contradicted forthwith by Mr. Lankester Harding, who said that he had the scrolls. We must wait for authoritative information and photostatic reproduction before we can speak with any confidence on the subject. But it certainly looks as if we must prepare ourselves for *Further Thoughts on the Dead Sea Scrolls.*

For the present, the opportunity presents itself to add a few notes on the preceding pages.

Pp. 15 ff. An excellent account of the discovery and purchase of the scrolls is given by Mr. Allegro in the first two chapters of his Pelican book, *The Dead Sea Scrolls*, published at the end of August.

P. 38, lines 7–17. In the Nahum commentary mentioned on p. 97, an interval of time is indicated "from Antiochus to the rise of the rulers of the Kitti'im"; this supports the identification of the Kitti'im with the Romans rather than with the followers of Antiochus.

P. 46, lines 7–9. So the Mandaeans of Iraq bury their dead (cf. p. 123).

P. 73, lines 14–17. The Seleucid kings are indeed said to have hired mercenaries from these coastlands ("isles"), but these were foreign troops, additional to their regular forces (I Macc. 6: 29; 11: 38). In I Macc. 15: 1 the expression "the isles of the sea" is used vaguely for Rhodes.

P. 73, lines 22–31. I should not dream of denying (as some

do) that the Seleucids had the same practice; but the evidence is stronger in the case of the Romans.

P. 75, lines 5–7. Some have dated the *Rule of War* in the Seleucid period, but the battle order described in it bears a much closer resemblance to that of the Romans in the first century B.C. than it does to the Macedonian phalanx.

P. 78, lines 29–37. Two or three lines before the beginning of this quotation from the *Rule of the Congregation* there is a mutilated sentence which seems to contain the words: "when [God] begets the Messiah with them" (cf. "today I have begotten you" in Psa. 2: 7).

P. 79, lines 18–20. The persons referred to in Psa. 105: 15 as "anointed ones" and "prophets" are the patriarchs (cf. Gen. 20: 7).

P. 81, line 4. The "Expounder of the Law" is more probably the successor of the Teacher of Righteousness as director of the community, who led the temporary migration to Damascus. Elsewhere in the *Admonition* (col. 6, line 7) the "staff" of Num. 21: 18 is interpreted of the Expounder of the Law. In a commentary on Isaiah, found in Cave 4, the title is given to an eschatological figure, contemporary with the Davidic Messiah.

P. 88, lines 23–25. The expression "the men of war" is probably figurative (borrowed from Deut. 2: 14), and need not refer to soldiers; the reference is possibly to those Pharisees who went into exile in the reign of Alexander Jannaeus and returned at the accession of Salome Alexandra.

P. 91, line 20. It must be remembered, however, that any high priest might be said to have "ruled in Israel", since the post-exilic high priest was *ex officio* head of the Jewish state.

P. 95, lines 6–8. It is probably the Pharisees who are referred to here and there in the Zadokite and Qumran texts as "seekers after smooth things" (an echo of Isa. 30: 10).

P. 95, lines 12–13. Professor Dupont-Sommer (*The Dead Sea Scrolls*, p. 37) suggests that this Absalom was Alexander's brother-in-law—not his own brother but his wife's brother, and therefore brother to Simeon Ben-Shetach, the Pharisaic leader. But we must resist the temptation to use this hypothesis as the foundation of another hypothesis!

P. 109, lines 10–12. In the later stages of removing their library to places of safety, they apparently had no time to wrap the manuscripts in linen and place them in jars, but were forced to deposit them in the caves just as they were.

P. 127, line 12. The words "there is no evidence" must of course refer to the time of writing these pages, and (like many other things in this book) may call for revision in the light of further information. In his Pelican book (p. 148) Mr. Allegro says that the Qumran sectaries gave to the expected priestly Messiah the names "Teacher of Righteousness" and "Interpreter of the Law", and infers from this that they believed the priestly Messiah would be the Teacher of Righteousness in resurrection. The relevant texts will be published soon, and their evidence can then be evaluated. But it is doubtful if the Teacher of Righteousness is identical with the "Interpreter of the Law"—or "Expounder of the Law", as the phrase has been rendered above (*cf.* pp. 81, 139).

P. 129, line 38. Of course, if one were writing historical fiction, it would be possible to explain that John had been excommunicated from the group and, in view of his stringent vows taken at initiation, was prevented from eating any other kind of food!

P. 133, lines 21 ff. We should bear in mind, however, that nearly every new discovery in the religious history of this general area has been hailed as providing the solution to "the problem of the Fourth Gospel"!

INDEX

Aaron, 77, 83, 88, 93, 101, 105, 127, 135
Abomination of desolation, 100
Absalom, house of, 95, 140
Acts of the Apostles, 57, 67, 80, 82, 86, 135, 136
Agrippa I, 12, 49
Agrippa II, 51
Ain Feshkha, 107
Albright, W. F., 19, 20, 23, 39, 133, 138
Alexander the Great, 11, 37, 73, 99
Alexander Jannaeus, 91 ff., 101, 139
Alexandria, 58, 66, 112, 113
Allegro, J. M., 97, 126, 138, 140
American Schools of Oriental Research, 18, 20, 21, 26
Ananias and Sapphira, 106
Angels, 116, 120
Antigonus, 49
Antioch, 99
Antiochus IV (Epiphanes), 12, 38, 42, 61, 65, 99, 119, 138
Antiochus VII (Sidetes), 49
Antipas, 106
Aqiba, 54, 57, 65, 67, 81
Arabic, 53, 57
Aramaic, 22, 27, 63
Archelaus, 12, 49, 108
Aristobulus I, 118
Aristobulus II, 91, 95
Assumption of Moses, 27
Assyria, 73
Atonement, 98, 102 f.
Atonement, Day of, 89, 97
Augustus, 49

Babylon, Babylonia, 11, 66
Baker, H. W., 29 f.
Balaam, 37, 54, 77, 78, 80
Baptism, baptisteries, 48, 106, 115, 120, 121, 123, 126, 129, 131, 134
Bar-Kokhba, 13, 53 ff., 56, 81
Barthélemy, D., 33
Bedouin, 15, 29, 39, 53, 56, 110, 138
Bel and the Dragon, 36
Belial, 75, 121
Ben-Sira, 59 f.
Bethlehem, 16
Biberkraut, J., 17
Birnbaum, S. A., 40, 41
British Museum, 24, 40
Brownlee, W. H., 20, 94, 130
Burrows, M., 20, 21, 23, 26, 62

Cairo, 32, 111
Calendar, 89
Camps, 85, 101, 105
Canon of O.T., 58 f.
Cave Sect, 110 f.
Celibacy, 46, 112, 113, 115, 121
Cemetery, 45, 46, 106
Chaldaeans, 36, 37, 71 f.
Christianity, Christians, 54, 55, 79 ff., 86, 96, 98, 106, 110, 123 ff.
Chronicles, Books of, 67
Claudius, 49
Clermont-Ganneau, C. S., 24, 39, 45
Coins, 49, 51, 52, 109, 118
Colossians, Epistle to, 57
Commentaries, 21, 28, 35 ff.
Commodus, 55
Community of goods, 106, 107, 113
Conflagration, 120 f.
Copper scrolls, 29 ff.
Corinthians, First Epistle to, 82
Covenant, New, 101, 134
Crucifixion, 97, 108
Cullmann, O., 123, 124, 127
Cyprus, 37
Cyrus, 11, 76, 130

Damascus, 32, 108, 139
Daniel, Book of, 27, 37, 58, 74, 99, 103, 104, 127
Dates, 19 f., 23 ff., 34 ff., 56 f.
David, Davidic dynasty, 11, 76, 77, 95, 135
Dead Sea, 15, 26, 45, 46, 50, 51, 53, 107, 112, 117, 121
Deuteronomy, Book of, 27. 55 56, 58, 65, 67, 68, 69, 74, 77, 80, 83, 115, 127, 132, 139
De Vaux, R., 26, 45, 113, 119
Discipline, 103, 105 f., 120
Driver, G. R., 24 f., 41, 42
Dualism, 104
Dupont-Sommer, A., 96, 119, 126, 128, 139

Earlier discoveries, 109 f.
Earthquake, 47, 48 f., 50, 108
Ebionites, 123 f.
Ecclesiasticus, Book of, 59 f.
École Biblique, 16, 26, 45
Egypt, 66, 73, 74, 75, 99

Eleazar Ben-Po'irah, 93, 94 f.
Elijah, 79, 80, 88, 127
Elisha, 79
En-gedi, 46, 50, 112, 119
Enoch, Book of, 31, 58
Essenes, 45, 46, 95, 112 ff., 129, 130, 134, 136 f.
Esther, Book of, 31, 58
Euripides, 57
Excommunication, 116, 140
Exodus, Book of, 27, 55, 56, 67, 68
Expounder of the Law, 81, 139, 140
Ezekiel, Book of, 27, 74, 79, 102, 134

Farmer, W. R., 107

Galilaeans, Galilee, 54, 55, 108, 126, 131, 135
Genesis, Book of, 27, 55, 56, 68, 139
Genesis, paraphrase of, 22, 40
Genizah, 17, 32, 111
Gerizim, Mt., 30
Geyser, A. S., 130
Gnosis, Gnosticism, 104, 123
Greek manuscripts, 53, 55, 56, 57, 65

Habakkuk, Book of, 35 f., 56, 58, 96
Habakkuk, commentary on, 21, 35 ff., 40, 70 ff., 85 ff., 88 ff., 94, 96
Hadrian, 53, 55
Harding, G. L., 15, 26, 27, 138
Hasidim, 99 ff., 118 f.
Hasmoneans, 12, 91, 101, 118
Hebrew language, 63 f.
Hebrew University, 16, 17, 21
Hebrews, Epistle to, 68, 82, 135
Hebron, 30
Hellenism, 99
Herod, 12, 49, 51, 55, 108
Herodias, 96
Hexapla, 110
Hezekiah, 59 f.
Hillel, 132
Hippolytus, 117 f., 120
Holy War, 74 ff., 103, 136
Hymns of Thanksgiving, 22, 87, 121
Hyrcanus II, 91, 95

Immortality, 114, 118
Initiation, 105 f., 115 f., 120
Ink, 41, 47
Inkwells, 47, 48
Inspectors, 105
Interpretation of Bible, 70 ff., 85, 87
Isaiah, Book of, 27, 34, 58, 59, 60, 61, 69, 76, 86, 98, 101, 102, 104, 130, 137, 139
Isaiah, commentary on, 139
Isaiah, manuscripts of, 16, 18, 19, 21, 22, 40, 55, 59 ff., 62, 63, 64
Israel, State of, 18, 21, 22

James the Just, 83
Jars, 15, 17, 27, 42, 43, 44, 45, 47, 109
Jeremiah, 27
Jericho, 42, 50, 109, 131
Jerome, 64
Jerusalem, 11, 12, 13, 16, 22, 30, 38, 50, 53, 58, 74, 75, 76, 80, 89, 91, 97, 100, 102, 108, 109, 112, 124
Jeshua (high priest), 11
Jewish Christians, 54, 55, 83, 123 f.
Job, Book of, 68
John (Baptist), 80, 83, 96, 108, 126, 128 ff., 140
John, Gospel of, 57, 80, 105, 128, 133, 134, 140
John Hyrcanus, 49, 61, 93, 101
Jordan (river and valley), 48, 50, 80, 121, 129, 131
Jordan, Kingdom of, 15, 26, 29
Josephus, 46, 49, 50, 73, 92, 93, 97, 112, 114 ff. ,117 f., 120 f., 123, 129
Joshua, Book of, 57
Jubilees, Book of, 22, 28, 31, 58, 89
Judæa, Wilderness of, 46, 128, 129, 131
Judah (Ben-Gedidiah), 93, 94
Judah (Essene), 95, 118
Judah, kings of, 46, 53
Judas Maccabaeus, 38, 100
Judges, Book of, 27
Judgment, 102 f., 129 f.
Justin, 81

Kenyon, F. G., 23, 69
Khirbet Mird, 57
Khirbet Qumran, 45 ff., 107, 108, 109, 113, 119, 126
Kidron, 57
Kings, Books of, 79
Kingship, 79, 84, 136
Kitti'im, 37, 38, 71, 72, 73, 75, 81, 86, 91, 92, 138
Knowledge, 104
Kuhn, K. G., 31

Lamech, Book of, 22
Lamps, 44
Levi, tribe of, 76, 77
Levites, 101, 105, 106, 135
Leviticus, Book of, 27, 138
Libby, W. F., 42
Light and darkness, 104, 133
Linen, 42 f., 109
Lippens, P., 26
Logos, 105
Luke, Gospel of, 57, 90, 92, 129, 130

Maccabean age, 61, 63, 65
Maccabees, Books of, 38, 65, 100
Macedonians, 11, 99, 139
Magnes, J. L., 17

Man of Falsehood, 71, 94
Mandaeans, 123, 138
Manual work, 107, 113, 116 f.
"Many (The)" 105, 120
Mark, Gospel of, 57, 80, 82, 103, 131, 132, 133
Marriage, 46, 106, 121, 132
Masada, 50 f., 112
Maskilim, 99 f., 101, 103, 104
Massoretes, Massoretic text, 23, 25, 56, 57, 61 ff.
Mattathias, 100
Matthew, Gospel of, 128, 134
Meals, common, 78, 106, 115, 116, 120
Melchizedek, 83, 135
Menelaus, 98, 99
Messiah, Messianism, 13, 54, 76 ff., 88, 96, 121, 126, 127, 128, 131, 134, 135, 136, 139, 140
Micah, Book of, 58
Micah, commentary on, 28, 87
Michael (archangel), 74, 75
Michel, A., 98
Milik, J. T., 33
Minor Prophets, 56, 58
Moabite Stone, 24, 63
Moffatt, J., 100
Morning Bathers, 122
Moses, 68, 77, 80, 81, 101, 118, 127, 134, 138
Mowry, L., 133
Murabba'at, 41, 53 ff., 61, 65, 66

Nabataean, 56
Nahum, Book of, 58
Nahum, commentary on, 97, 138
Nash papyrus, 19, 20
Nebuchadrezzar, 11
Nero, 49, 51
Nestorians, 110
Nicodemus, 134
Nicolas of Damascus, 55
Noah, Book of, 28
Numbers, Book of, 54, 56, 77, 81

Oaths, 115, 117
Oil, 117
Onias III (high priest), 98
Onias (rain-maker), 95
Origen, 109 f.
Ostraca, 55

Palaeography, 38 ff., 57
Palaeo-Hebrew (Phoenician) script, 27, 40, 46, 53, 68
Palestine Museum, 32, 45
Paul, 24
Pella, 124
Persians, 11, 44, 99
Peter, 80, 86, 104
Petrie, W. M. F., 43
Phalanx, 139
Pharisees, 89, 93, 95, 101, 102, 119, 122, 132, 136, 139
Philo, 112 ff., 118, 121
Phylacteries, 55 f.
Plenderleith, H. J., 39 f., 41
Pliny the Elder, 46, 112, 113, 115, 119, 121
Ploeg, J. van der, 16
Pompey, 38, 97
Pottery, 43, 46, 47
Priesthood, priests, 11, 12, 77 ff., 83, 84, 91, 101, 105 f., 115, 116, 129, 135, 136, 139
Procurators of Judæa, 49
Prophecy, prophets, 77, 79, 80, 84, 86, 104, 120, 136
Psalms, Book of, 27, 56, 58, 79, 81, 82, 83, 109, 138, 139
Psalms, commentaries on, 28
Psalms of Joshua, 77
Ptolemies, 11, 73, 99

Qaraites, 110 f.
Qirqisani, 110 f.
Qumran, 15, 29, 31, 32, 34, 35, 37, 41, 43, 45 ff., *et passim*
Qumran community, 46, 47, 61, 66, 68, 70, 74 f., 79, 83, 84, 85, 87, 89, 90 f., 92, 96, 98, 99 ff., 112 f., 119, 123 ff.

Radiocarbon test, 42 f.
Renan, E., 136
Resurrection, 88, 98, 118, 127
Revelation, Book of, 70, 81
Revised Standard Version, 62, 63, 68
Romans, 12, 38, 42, 47, 50, 51, 52, 53, 54, 55, 73, 91, 108, 109, 116, 123, 124, 138, 139
Rowley, H. H., 38, 48, 98
Rule of the Community, 20, 22, 31, 32, 40, 59, 77, 78, 104, 106, 120, 129
Rule of the Congregation, 78, 139
Rule of War, 22, 73 ff., 78, 81, 82, 139
Ruling of manuscripts, 41

Sabbath, 113, 116, 118, 120, 133
Sacrifices, 102, 115, 121, 135
Sadducees, 89, 110
Salome Alexandra, 91, 139
Samaritan text, 66, 68, 69
Sampsaeans, 117
Samuel, Archbishop A. Y., 16, 17, 19, 20, 21
Samuel, Books of, 27, 67
Sanhedrin, 80
Schoeps, H. J., 124
Scriptorium, 57, 48
"Seekers after smooth things", 139

Seleucids, 11, 12, 73, 93, 99, 100, 139
Sennacherib, 86
Septuagint, 23, 36, 56, 62, 65 ff., 79
Servant of Yahweh, 61, 62 f., 84, 98, 102 f., 131, 136
Shammai, 132
Shapira, M. W., 22, 39, 45
Simeon Ben-Shetach, 93, 94, 139
Simon Maccabaeus, 93, 101
Simonides, C., 39
Smith, W. R., 60
Smyth, K., 125
Solomon, 11
Son of Man, 103, 136
Sowmy, B., 18
Spirits, the two, 104
Star (out of Jacob), 54, 77, 78, 80, 81
Stephen, 80
Sukenik, E. L., 16, 17, 18, 22, 23, 28, 39, 119
Sunrise, 116, 117
Synagogues, 120
Syria, 73, 99
Syriac, 57
Syrian Monastery, 16, 21, 40

Ta'amireh, 15, 57
Tabernacles, Feast of, 92 f.
Talmud, 93, 94, 95, 110, 132
Teacher of Righteousness, 61, 71, 81, 85 ff., 101, 102, 104, 108, 118, 119, 126, 127, 128, 131, 136, 139, 140
Teicher, J. L., 96, 123, 125 f.
Temple, 11, 12, 73, 80, 89, 91, 97, 100, 102, 115, 135
Temptation, 128, 131
Testament of Levi, 28, 31, 76
Testaments of the Twelve Patriarchs, 76
Text of O.T., 23, 56, 57, 61 ff.
Tiberius, 49
Tischendorf, C., 39
Titus (emperor), 51, 73
Tobiads, 98
Tobit, Book of, 31
Trajan, 52, 56
Trever, J. C., 18, 20, 22, 40
Trypho, 81
Tyre, 49

Urim and Thummim, 77, 105
Uzziah, 46

Vespasian, 50, 52, 109
Vesuvius, 112
Vows, 106, 115 f.
Wadi en-Nar, 57
War, 12, 49, 50, 51, 52, 53 ff., 74 ff., 103, 108 f., 121, 136
Weis, P. R., 111
Wheeler, M., 42
Wicked Priest, 71, 89 ff.
Wilson, E., 125, 126
Wisdom, Book of, 57
Wisdom literature, 104
Women, 46, 106

Yeshua Ben-Galgolah, 54

Zadok, Zadokite dynasty, 11, 12, 30, 32, 98, 99, 105
Zadokite work, 32, 78, 79, 81, 85, 87, 88, 108, 111, 132, 139
Zealots, 108, 117
Zeitlin, S., 24
Zephaniah, commentary on, 28
Zoroastrianism, 120

L.I.F.E. College Library
1100 Glendale Blvd.
Los Angeles, Calif. 90026

L.I.F.E. College Library
1100 Glendale Blvd.
Los Angeles, Calif. 90026